Recommendations:

William Carey, Hudson Taylor, Amy Carmichael, C.T. Studd, Lottie Moon, Jim Elliot...what was it that caused them to leave homeland, family, wealth and comfort to be Christ's arms of love to the darkest and most distant parts of the earth? A passion for the things on God's heart permeated their lives. Writing from his own passion for Christ, John Zumwalt communicates this passion in 21 short chapters filled with mission stories, concepts and scriptures that will set your heart on fire with God's love for a desperately needy world.

Rev. Philip S. Bogosian,
Director International Adopt-A-People Campaign

John Zumwalt's book serves as a pointed reminder of the eternal value that Jesus Christ places upon a lifestyle of SACRIFICE, URGENCY and BROKENNESS on behalf of the unreached. I urge you to read it and in the process allow God to ruin you for anything less!

Rev. David Smithers
Editor, The Watchword Revival Resource Center

John has an evident passion not only after the heart of God, but also after this lost world. That passion is communicated in this timely book.

Rev. Ray Comfort
Author of Hell's Best Kept Secret

No one articulates the mission message of the Heart of God like John Zumwalt. This book is fresh with illustrations that clearly bring God's Word to real life. You will be changed to a deeper walk with Jesus and a greater compassion for the lost. It is presented with zest and enthusiasm. It is a quick read that packs a huge punch. Here, missions is more than theory, theology or testimony. John awakens us to the passion of God that all peoples know Jesus. You and your church will never be the same after reading this book.

James L. West
God Ministries

It would be rare and wonderful ▮▮▮▮▮▮▮▮▮▮ sy to read and
highly arresting in its advance ▮▮▮▮▮▮▮▮▮▮ es. **This is it.**
John Zumwalt has made a signi

Dr. Ralph D. Winter
Founder, U.S. Center for World Missions
President, William Carey International University

iii

As one who has been working to fulfill the Great Commission in Asia for nearly 35 years, one of my off-the-continent challenges (and sometimes frustrations) has been to promote the cause of missions. *Passion for the Heart of God* does just this and is, therefore, a very welcome tool and encouragement to me. Its informative statistics, facts and stories--yes, lots of great stories!--should get anyone excited and serious about God's passion!

Rev. David Wang
President, Asian Outreach International Ltd.

A book full of surprises and fresh insights. Every chapter was chocked full of startling and exciting revelations! I will never read my Bible the same. You cannot help but read this and fall in love with our great God, reviving the excitement, conviction and zeal of first love. As a missionary, I can think of no better book to give my friends and family. Every pastor, mission committee member, every church member will find this book indispensable in discovering the plans of our God for this unique time in history!

Name withheld
Missionary in 'closed' country

Passion for the Heart of God is empowering, inspiring and equipping. John Zumwalt is a forerunner of the missional part of God's heart. If you're hungry to know God's Heart and His desire for people all over the world to know Him, then reading this will be like throwing a match on gasoline.

Charlie Hall
Generation Music

John's command of Biblical teaching with refreshing insights and amazing real-life stories is powerful. What is refreshing about this book is the white-hot passion it conveys for people who will go to hell without ever having heard the name of Jesus. Not only that, but the fact that this passion is God's passion, and it is one we can share with Him. I highly recommend this book to every Christian who wants to be after God's own heart.

Rev. Nate Wilson
Church Mobilization Specialist, Caleb Project

Passion for the Heart of God

John Willis Zumwalt

HGM Publishing
a division of Heart of God Ministries
3720 S. Hiwassee Rd., Choctaw, OK 73020

Copyright © 2000 by John W. Zumwalt
International Standard Book Number: 0-9679781-0-6
All rights reserved. The author retains international copyright. Written permission must be secured from the publisher to use or reproduce any part of this book, except for brief quotations in critical reviews or articles.

Printed in the United States of America
Published by HGM Publishing
3720 S. Hiwassee Rd.
Choctaw, OK 73020-6128
Second Printing: July 2001
Third Printing: September 2002
Fourth Printing: November 2004
Fifth Printing: August 2005
Sixth Printing: January 2007
Seventh Printing: January 2009
Eighth Printing: March 2013

Unless otherwise noted, Scripture references are from the *New King James Version* Copyright ©1982 , Thomas Nelson, Inc.

(Italics or bolded words are for emphasis by author.)

"There is a great passion burning in the **heart of God**. It is tenderly warm and tenaciously strong. Its fires never burn low, nor lose their fine glow. That passion is to win man back home again. The whole world of man is included in its warm, eager reach.

This is a *love* passion, a passion of love. And love itself is the master passion of both the human heart and of **God's heart**. Nothing can grip and fill and sway the heart either of man or God like that.

It is an overmastering passion, the *overmastering* passion of **God's heart**. It has guided and controlled all His thoughts and plans for man from the first. The purpose of winning man, and the whole race, back again is the dominant gripping passion of **God's heart** today. Everything is made to bend to this one end."

S.D. Gordon[1]

1. S. D. Gordon, What It Will Take to Change the World (Grand Rapids: Baker Book House, 1979) p. 1.

Dedication

To Three Pioneer Missionaries

Willis Hosmer Zumwalt, the first real live missionary I ever met, who taught me about apostolic tenacity, who refused to be side-tracked by lucrative financial offers and by those who would dissuade Him because he was too old or didn't have the right kind of education, who fought through the greatest challenges, learned several of the world's hardest languages, overcame the impossible obstacles and physical difficulties to obey the high calling of Christ. My Dad has always been my hero.
"I didn't have what others had, so I had to
work twice as hard and long."

Boyd Aitken, who gave up a brilliant career in British soccer, to follow Jesus to the frontiers of Borneo. It was he who recognized God calling me into ministry, while I was still in high school, and taught me apostolic motivation.
"Oh the deep, deep love of Jesus."

Alan Bemo, who taught me apostolic ambition, by never being satisfied with what he has done, nor where he has been, but has continued to press the frontier, to go where Christ has not yet been named, for the Glory of God and the salvation of man.
"I don't know what I have done, really."

May many more Apostles of your same Tenacity, Motivation and Ambition be released to the frontiers.

FOREWORD

When I first met John Zumwalt, I knew immediately that I would like him. He communicated clearly to me one thing, he was willing to be different. But he wasn't different for the mere sake of being different; he was different for the sake of the Kingdom. John knew then what the majority of the Body of Christ still needs to learn about now. Today a revolution is needed; a revolution that needs to take place in the Church, not only in America, but around the world; a revolution that gets people's focus off of themselves and on to God and His glory; a revolution where once again, man will serve God, not God serve man; a revolution that will move the Church to take our Father's glory to all of the nations on the face of the earth. In John's insightful book, *Passion for the Heart of God*, John gives a creative challenge to the Church to pursue God's heart to the ends of the earth. His stories are fresh, energizing and easy to read, but best of all, he holds nothing back. John challenges us all to become a part of the needed revolution. I highly encourage anyone in the Body of Christ to read this book.

Bob Sjogren
President, UnveilinGLORY
Author, *Unveiled At Last* and
Run With the Vision

CONTENTS

Introduction

"The secret of Christianity is not asking Jesus into your heart;
it is Jesus asking us into **His heart**."
Jamie Zumwalt

The heat was stifling. All the windows and doors had been sealed tight. Hours earlier we had nailed them shut and placed boards over the openings insuring no gaps. This was the only way we could keep a grenade from being dropped into the church while we slept. As I looked up at the slowly rotating fan, trying to get comfortable on the hard floor, I was sure that I was about to die. I was only 19 years old and had thought a short-term mission trip to the Golden Triangle would be fun.

The hills of Northern Thailand were exciting, yet deadly. Opium fields of beautiful poppies gave color to breathtaking landscapes marred by the harsh reality of warlord violence and opium addiction. Ethnic nationalism and tribal rivalries had turned the Golden Triangle into a death zone of misery and terror. I was sure that I was to be its next victim. I cried out to Jesus, "I am too young to die!" His soothing Holy Spirit came up beside me and whispered, "John, you will die. Now decide whom you will die for: Your own little adventure or Me and My Name's sake?" I decided, fully expecting never to leave Thailand alive, to make whatever life I had left, count for Him.

That was the beginning for me. The next morning Jesus began to rewrite my life. I had been heading toward a career in art, and He adjusted that. As I awoke the next day, He began to show me His heart, and I began to feel His heart in me, working through my emotions and desires, my passions and ambitions. In those mountain jungles filled with hatred and murder, Jesus was freeing opium addicts, and filling churches with the tongues, tribes and nations He so loves. In the midst of horrible opposition, threats and martyrdom, Jesus was establishing His Kingdom!

This book is an introduction to some of the issues that burn in the heart of God. It is as important a study as one can begin. My wife once said, "The secret of Christianity is not asking Jesus into your heart; it is Jesus asking us into His heart." He wants to mature us past our inviting Him to be involved in our life and dreams. He is inviting us to be involved in His life and dreams.

The information contained in this book is not wholly a product of my own scholarship. Occasionally one comes up with an idea he or she is sure is original, only to discover on some forgotten bookshelf another who also has made this discovery. I have been in the missions world for over twenty-seven years, and have heard much, been influenced by many, and of my own have probably generated very little original thought in these pages. That credit lies completely with wonderful men and women of God such as: Ralph D. Winter and his wife, Roberta, Don Richardson, Bob Sjogren, Walter Kaiser, Bill and Amy Sterns, Steven Hawthorne, and my good friend and mobilizer, Boyd Morris, who was first used by God to open my eyes to the scriptures, the world and the glorious hope that is ours in Christ Jesus.

I want to thank the ladies at El Oasis in Mexico who housed us and prayed us through all kinds of spiritual attack, while I was in the process of writing this book. Then, there are so many who have read this book and volunteered their time and energy in giving correction and input. I thank you for your support of me in this endeavor.

Finally, I want to thank my wife, Jamie, who has toiled long and hard to see this book through. Without her this would have never happened. My advice to all is marry someone who will make you look good. I married well.

one

Taking His Name in Vain

"God is so pleased when He
finds **His heart** beating in another."[1]
Steven C. Hawthorne

Putting Jesus Back in the Manger

When my first child, Jessica, turned one, we celebrated by letting her eat cake and ice cream for the first time. Up until this birthday we had done our best to keep her from sweets, but now she gleefully smeared dessert all over her face while grabbing whole handfuls of chocolate cake. Each birthday, we try to focus on what is meaningful to the person we celebrate. We give gifts that we think they will like. We even try to surprise the recipient.

In ten years, it would be fairly unsuitable for me to give my daughter a teething ring or a rattle. She will not have any use for those. It is never improper to remember how cute she was as a baby, but it would be terribly inappropriate for us to celebrate her as though she still was one.

It is always interesting to me that at Christmas time the event of Jesus' *birth* is the center of focus, rather than Jesus *Himself!* You may say that everything *does* focus on Jesus. No, all attention is on *Baby* Jesus: looking at His pictures, reenacting the delivery, singing about drums and donkeys. We do not focus on Jesus, the Ever-living One. He is no longer that cute, harmless infant, representing peace and love, lying in the hay. I am convinced that we celebrate the *Baby* Jesus, because He is not a threat. In case we have forgotten, the manger is empty, and Jesus is all grown up.

During our church Christmas pageant, part way through the program, one junior high girl realized to her horror that the manger was empty. She desperately ran across the stage and down to where the "Jesus-look-alike" baby doll lay, grabbed it, ran back to the stage and deftly placed Jesus where He 'belonged.'

Are we in the Church guilty of pushing Jesus, the King of the Universe, back into the manger, so that we can feel secure and relieved, non-threatened? How is it that we can get everyone to bow at the manger, but they ignore the Man who is worthy of our worship? The whole world seems eager to bow before the Jesus who is quiet, peaceful, and yes, non-threatening, while the grown up version repulsively demands obedience.

The *Baby* Jesus does not challenge our culture, but the adult Jesus does. When a man asked Jesus how he could get into heaven, Jesus did not lead him in a simple sinner's prayer. Instead, He told the man to sell everything and give it to the poor. The real Jesus, who is all grown up, is not so easy to love. He offends common sense and cultural norms. Someone says, "I want to follow you," and Jesus replies, "I have no place to lay my head." Another says, "Let me serve you," and God commands, "Leave your father, home, your people and culture, and go to the land I will show you." (Gen. 12:1-3)

American Christianity, in exchanging true worship for this infant adoration, is in shambles. We sing songs like "I've got a River of Life flowing out of me, makes the lame to walk and the blind to see, opens prisons' doors, sets the captives free. I've got a River of Life flowing out of me." Yet few of us have ever seen God move like that, let alone through us. We are living a shallow, hollow Christianity and hardly realize it. Our Christianity looks nothing like the Book of Acts, and we somehow have no problem with that. It is anemic and weak compared to the apostolic glory days. We have started to rewrite our theology based on our lack of experience, rather than based upon the scriptures. Pretty soon our theology will be such that scriptural admonitions will not apply, and its examples will be considered isolated and irrelevant.

Most denominations in North America are disguising the fact that their North American growth is in the negatives by hiding it behind great statistical growth in the two-thirds world. If we do have a church that is growing in our city, it is almost always transfer growth. In other words, it is growing at the expense of other churches, rather than by converts. How can this be?

We have forgotten who our God is. I am not talking about symbolically including Him by a prayer before school, or a cross on a city seal or by reenacting His birth once a year. I am talking about forgetting the man: Jesus. Our worship and giving is often inappropriate, because we do not know who He is or what He desires. We must purposefully rediscover who our God is, because we have abandoned Him. We are no longer people who have abandoned ourselves to Him. We are not people after His heart.

What is the Heart of God?

What is the Heart of God? The Heart of God is His nature, His character, His passion, His purpose, His longings, His desires and His ambitions. It is what He dreams about, what His goals and intentions are, what His interests are, what brings a smile to His face and what can drive Him to anger. It is His emotional center. This is the Heart of God.

Some would prefer to think of God as not having an emotional side, at least not one that we can affect. But even as an obedient child brings joy to my heart and a disobedient child brings pain and sometimes a hint of rejection to my heart, so God rejoices and suffers over us like a parent.

> The LORD thy God in the midst of thee is mighty; he will save, **he will rejoice over thee with joy**; he will rest in his love, **he will joy over thee with singing** (Zeph. 3:17 KJV).

> O Jerusalem, Jerusalem, you who kill the prophets and stone those sent to you, how **often I have longed** to gather your children together, as a hen gathers her chicks under her wings, but you were not willing! (Luke 13:34 NIV)

> As he approached Jerusalem and saw the city, **he wept over it and said**, "If you, even you, had only known on this day what would bring you peace, but now it is hidden from your eyes" (Luke 19:41 NIV).

> Therefore **My heart yearns for him**; I will surely have mercy on him, says the Lord (Jer. 31:20).

He is deeply touched by our lives. His heart breaks for the lost and celebrates with the one coin that is found! Is there any doubt that He is the Father who rejoices over the prodigal? Our God is a passionate and emotional God! We affect Him. Few things bring happiness
to a Father's heart like seeing His child pursue the things that are close to His heart. Oh, that we would all be "chips off the ol' block."

What this generation of Christians needs, more than any other thing, is to know who God is. We need not to continue to treat Him as though He is a baby, but we need to find out what makes Him tick now. If you want to please Him, find out what He wants! How do you know what He wants? Learn His heart, and you will know the Person of God. When we find His heart, then, and only then, will we once again "smell" like the first century Christians - men and women after God's heart!

In his book *Desire of all Nations*, Egbert Smith wrote:

> To be like Christ is the aim and longing of every true child of
> God. A growing likeness to Him is the sure proof that our names
> are written in the Lamb's Book of Life. And to be Christlike
> we must get away from our selfishness and narrowness. We
> must emulate the big-heartedness of Him who died for all men.
> Sympathy with Christ's great heart and purpose is the supreme
> essential of Christlikeness; not Bible reading; not church-going;
> not saying prayers; not giving a tenth; not holding an orthodox
> creed. These are five splendid helps to Christlikeness. But they
> are not the real thing. Many a time they are substitutes for the
> real thing. The Pharisees had all five. Yet they showed a total,
> ghastly, damning unlikeness to Christ. Likeness to Him means
> sympathy with His great heart and purpose. That way spiritual
> life lies; that way Christlikeness lies; and no other way.
>
> We may be church members. We may preach in His Name,
> and in His Name cast out devils, and in His Name do many
> wonderful works. But we shall never be like Him, so long as we
> absorb ourselves in some narrow circle and turn a deaf ear to
> the cry of the unreached. Because Christ was the very opposite
> of that.[2]

Taking His Name in Vain

"Don't cuss . . . it's vulgar, and besides you shouldn't take the Lord's name in
vain," a thousand mothers have screamed . . . and then threatened a bar of soap.
If that were all there was to it, then we would have already mastered this original
member of the Ten Commandments.

As a *Christ*ian (which really means a "little Christ" or a "little anointed one"), this
becomes a troubling issue. Much like marriage, the two are becoming one: Jesus
and me. When people see me, they see all they know of Christ. I am the human
representative of Christ, much like an ambassador. But more than that, He lives in
me, and I am His body — His hands and His feet.

Rev. Hal Perkins, my friend and former pastor, explained it to me this way; "The
Lord's Name is His nature and character. When we take His Name, we take His
nature, His character, as our identity." It is not so much that we need to put on a
show for the world, but that the world will honor or despise the Name of Jesus
because of our lives. If we claim to know Him, yet persist in sin and self-rule,
Christ is shamed, and we have taken the Name of the Lord in vain. However, if
we walk in the Spirit and live a life of His love and His holiness, then His Name
is known and honored everywhere.

4

One premise for this book is that you are a sincere seeker of God. You are a *Christ*ian. You are one who is interested in obeying Christ at all costs. You understand that Jesus is Lord and has the right to rule in every thought, every decision and every emotion of your life. You are one whom the Scriptures call not just a "hearer" but a "doer" of the Word.

As we are searching for the Heart of God, it is important for us to stop kidding ourselves about what thoughts, actions and attitudes are from Him and which are of the flesh and habit. The Bible warns sternly, "Don't act thoughtlessly, but try to find out and do whatever
the Lord wants you to" (Eph. 5:17 TLB).

As you discover what His heart is all about and are startled to realize that you are in opposition or indifferent to those items, you need to repent. It is not God who needs to come around to our way of thinking. It is we who need to confess, "Jesus I don't feel that way. I know I should, but I don't. I don't want to take your name in vain. Please change me, so that I will be like you."

Oh, we are your fuel, Lord.
Oh, set our hearts in a blaze.
Oh, wherever you say we'll go, Lord.
We'll take up our cross and suffer loss
For the sake of the Name.
A vision of the world aflame,
Across the globe is written Jesus' Name.
And the heart of God is burning
In the hearts of His people.³

Notes
1. Steven C. Hawthorne, "Wisdom for the Window: Practical Training For Prayer Journeyers" (Colorado Springs: Christian Information Network, 1995).
2. Egbert W. Smith, *The Desire of All Nations* (Garden City: Doubleday, Doran and Company, Inc., 1928), pp. 14-15.
3. Charlie Hall, "The Vision," Generation Productions, 1997.

two

Turtles in the Road

"We will not be able to seek the mind of the Lord
until we receive His heart."[1]
Loren Cunningham

It was late, and I was on my way back to southern Idaho, where I was in my third year of studies at Northwest Nazarene College. My car wheels grazed the lane-dividing bumps (whatever they are called) sending the thump, thump sound to my ears and that vibration to my body, reminding me to stay in my lane.

My wife thought she knew what those bumps were called. As a kid, someone had told her that those were turtles in the road, and every time you ran over one you killed it. I knew that was not true. Funny what some people say. No, I knew that the highway department had placed those bumps there so that blind people can drive. I went along for a mile with my eyes kind of closed, wondering how hard it would be to be blind and drive (yes, I was in college - amazing who they will let in) when suddenly I started wondering how they would know when to get off the freeway . . . or if a car was stopped ahead of them . . . and before I knew it another assumption, placed there by some adult prankster in my early years, met its embarrassing end.

Most people get rid of these half-truths and outlandish lies before I shamefully did. How strange it would be to have adults all entrenched with their various stories made up to understand what those bumps in the road are and why they have been placed there. Yet, in the realm of Christianity this is precisely what we daily encounter - a bit of truth mixed with human logic or only half the truth, giving an incomplete and misleading picture.

For instance, has the pastor at the end of a service ever blessed you with the benediction, "May God be gracious to us and bless us and make His face shine upon us . . ."? He may raise one hand, or even both, but the blessing is incomplete

7

and not biblical, in the sensethat he is quoting Psalm 67:1 and leaving the sentence and thought incomplete. David the psalmist was not saying, "Oh bless us and be close and intimate with us, so we can just enjoy you." No, the verse continues:

> May God be gracious to us and bless us and make his face
> shine upon us, **that your ways may be known on earth, your**
> **salvation among all nations.**

There is a reason that we need His blessings and intimacy, that we might be a testimony to the ends of the earth. It is not just about us and what we get out of it. It is about the nations and their salvation. Through us, God desires to affect the remotest corners of the world.

Many of us, sadly, have only heard the first part of the verse. Why? The verse does not end with *bless us.* It has a comma and then clearly goes on to pray that through us God can bless the ends of the earth. Perhaps many pastors do not include the second part, because they do not perceive it to be much of a blessing. Nevertheless, it is not just for us, but through us to the whole world.

> May God be gracious to us and bless us and make his face shine
> upon us, that your ways may be known on earth, your salvation
> among all nations. May the peoples praise you, O God; may all
> the peoples praise you. May the nations be glad and sing for joy,
> for you rule the peoples justly and guide the nations of the earth.
> May the peoples praise you, O God; may all the peoples praise
> you. Then the land will yield its harvest, and God, our God, will
> bless us. God will bless us, and all the ends of the earth will fear
> him (Ps. 67).

Can you finish this verse: "Be still and know . . . "? You know it, right? It is a favorite worship song for many. "Be still and know that I am God . . ." Sadly, the song continues to repeat this first half of Psalm 46:10 over and over again, and few people ever learn the exciting second half:

> Be still, and know that I am God; **I will be exalted among**
> **the nations, I will be exalted in the earth.**

This is a verse of assurance to those of us who doubt that the missionary task will ever be accomplished. *"Yes it will, for I am God. Where now there is war between the nations and myself, I will bring reconciliation, and there will be peace. Though you see them bowing to idols and imprisoned by demonic lies, some day all the peoples of the world will exalt me!"*

How sad that in only knowing half of the verse, we have been cheated of this great

Truth. You will find as you go through your Bible that much of what you have underlined and studied have been half verses or half ideas. It is only natural to meditate on the verses that make us feel good and bless us, but look again. Is there a reason God is blessing you, beyond the warm fuzzy you receive?

Back to School

The great preacher, Charles Haddon Spurgeon, knew that the Bible would always surprise us. He said, "Nobody ever outgrows scripture; the book widens and deepens with our years."[2] If our hearts are set correctly, then we are able to learn anew from the Holy Spirit every morning. As the Chinese proverb states so well, we should aspire to "live to an old age and learn to an old age." May we never arrive at the port of knowing it all; may we continue on the journey of exploration and discovery of our God through His Word.

I grew up as a missionary kid, but my idea was, as Bob Sjogren, cofounder of Frontiers, has described with tongue in cheek, that Jesus did all His important teaching, died, was resurrected, was about ready to go back to heaven and He said, *"Oh, I can't believe I forgot to tell you this. By the way, why don't you try and get some ethnic diversity in this thing we're going to call the Church and occupy yourself with that for a while, and I'll be back later."*[3] That is almost the idea I got. It was a tag-on on the end of Jesus' teaching, not central, not important. Our church programs, budgets and our personal priorities all seem to confirm the peripheral nature of Jesus' last command. But that is not the way it is in scripture, that is not the way it is in His heart, and like my wife's turtles, the old misconceptions had to give way to Truth. In this study, we are going to back up and look at the entire Bible and see God's emphasis for every tongue, tribe and nation.

> There are so many things to occupy our minds: so many books, so many examples, so many good teachings that deserve our attention, that say, "Here is a truth." But, as I have been serving the Lord these past years, He has led me to seek for two things and two things only; to know the heart of God in Christ and to know my own heart in Christ's light...

> Jesus loves people—all people, especially those society ignores. Therefore, I must know exactly how far He would travel for men, for that is the same distance He would journey again through me! I must know His thoughts concerning illness, poverty and human suffering! As His servant, I am useless to Him unless I know these things. If I would actually do His will, I must truly know His heart. Therefore, in all my study and times of prayer I am seeking for more than just knowledge; I am searching for the heart of God.[4]

Notes

1. Loren Cunningham, *Christian Growth Study Bible,* (Grand Rapids: Zondervan Bible Publishers, 1997).

2. Frank S. Mead, *Encyclopedia of Religious Quotations,* (London: Peter Davies Ltd., 1965), p. 33.

3. Bob Sjogren, *Unveiled At Last,* (Seattle: Youth With a Mission Publishing, 1992), pp. 64-65.

4. Francis Frangipane, *Holiness, Truth and the Presence of God*, (Cedar Rapids: Arrow Publications, 1986), pp. 22-23.

three

The Great Covenant

"The counsel of the Lord stands forever
The plans of **His heart** from generation to generation."
Psalm 33:11

The Beginning

David Hunter was faced with a dilemma for which Bible College had not prepared him. At the time, he was relatively a new missionary to a tribe of people who had not before heard the good news of salvation. Part of his message to his adopted people had been the promise of eternal life, and now one of his first converts was dead. The non- Christians claimed the spirits had taken her in punishment for leaving the gods of her fathers. The few other believers — all of them new in the faith — were wavering. What was he to tell them?

Since the deceased woman was a Christian, representatives from her village wanted David to perform whatever ceremony for the dead that Christians perform. He agreed, but as he canoed down the river to the village, he pondered his dilemma. How could he preach about eternal life over a dead body? He arrived at the village still uncertain about what to say, and he made his way through the restless crowd of villagers. Praying one last time for wisdom, he stepped into the hut where the dead woman lay.

As David faced the expectant group of people circled around their departed relative, God brought to his mind some scripture. He quoted these words:

After this I looked and there before me was a great multitude that no one could count, from every nation, tribe, people and language, standing before the throne and in front of the Lamb. They were wearing white robes and were holding palm branches in their hands. And they cried out in a loud voice:

"Salvation belongs to our God, who sits on the throne, and to the Lamb." Rev. 7:9-10

Triumphantly David turned to the people. "Today," he declared, "this tribe has its first representative before the throne of God. Up to this time you had no one there, but now you do!" David paused to let this announcement sink in. In the silence, the villagers began to assimilate what he had said, and then, as if on cue, everyone burst into joy and dancing. *For the first time in their history they were represented before the throne of God![1]*

The End in Sight

You remember when the Church was red hot. In AD 100, the Church was stirring it up. They were turning the world upside down. The apostles were zealots, willing to risk everything. You also know the sorry state the Church is in now, compared to that time. Back then, when they were turning the world upside down, there were 360 non-Christians for every Bible-believing Christian. That means that if the task were divided equally, each Christian was responsible for 360 non-Christians.

What do you think the number is today? I have heard many different responses to this question. Recently I was at a Bible College, and I asked it. The students answered 500,000 to one, one million to one. Their paradigm was all messed up. The real number is less than seven non-Christians for every true, Bible-believing Christian. If you were to measure everyone on planet earth that says, "Oh yeah, I'm a Christian" (There are a lot of them. Never mind that they have never been to church.), it would be approximately one to four. We are winning. I want you to get this picture. Have we won yet? No, but we are winning. What is happening on planet earth is astonishing!

David Wang, President of Asian Outreach, was at a dinner hosted by the government officials in China celebrating Chairman Mao's birthday. A Minister of Population Control complained that despite all efforts to control population with the one child policy, still every three weeks, one million people were added in China. Feeling unusual freedom, David bragged to her, "According to our research, followers of Jesus in China are growing at the rate of 20,000 a day!" A Minister of Internal Affairs leaned over and replied, "According to our government research, it's more like 30,000 believers a day!"[2]

Indonesia will not even publish the statistics on how many have become Christian over the last thirty years. Some say that around 25% of the population in Indonesia is Christian.[3] Why is this a big secret? Indonesia is a Muslim country. There has not been a breach in Islam like this in the entire world. Part of the reason is that a Bible College there, in order to graduate, requires the students to have converted fifteen Muslims to Christ and have planted one church among the Muslims. They alone can account for over 140,000 conversions.[4] We ought to do that for our Bible Colleges here. *You have studied the stuff, but can you do it?*

We used to call Africa "The Dark Continent." It had nothing to do with the color of their skin, but it was because of the condition of their hearts. Africa was about 3% Christian at the turn of the century. Now sub-Sahara Africa is 50% Christian — "the Continent of Light." At the turn of the century, Koreans were so resistant to the Gospel that Korea was called "impenetrable." Now above 30% of South Korea is Christian. Whenever the Koreans plant a church in Seoul, they place a red, neon cross on top of the building. When one flies into Seoul at night, a red glow can be seen coming from the city.[5]

God is accomplishing His goal all over the earth, even in places we like to hate. I wonder, are you praying for Iran? If you were to fly into Tehran and get into a taxi, you might see a little cross hanging from the rear view mirror. It has become a fad in Tehran. You might ask the driver if he is a Christian, and his response would be, "No, I'm a Muslim, but I would be if I could." They have no concept that they can convert. They were born a Muslim. In their minds, that is just the way it is, but they really like *Isa* (Jesus). The Qu'ran says that He is the sinless one, that He is the Word of God. It says that He is the one that God preserved to judge the world on the last day. He is the only "prophet" who can raise the dead and heal the sick.

If you were to go down to Baluchistan, which is in southern Iran and Pakistan, the people are a mixture of Persians and former African slaves. They are hated and very poor. You could go into a teashop where there are ten men sitting and say, "I'm here to teach you about Isa." Two will walk away uninterested. Eight will say, "Tell us more about Isa." Iran is more accepting of the Gospel than our western neighborhoods. That is because it is Good *News*. The essence of news is that it is new. They have never heard it before. Our neighbors have heard it over and over again.

Jim West, my Father-in-love and the Executive Director of Heart of God Ministries, was a pastor in the United States for about twenty years. He dragged cows, sheep, goats, a horse and donkey onto his church lawn to get people interested in the Christmas story. My wife and I invited him to visit us in Taiwan over the Christmas holiday. We went caroling through the village, and he told the Christmas story at each home, while I translated for him. There was one woman, who upon hearing the story, broke down weeping and asked, "Is it true? Could it be true?" Later Jim said, "For twenty years, I've been letting animals poop on the front lawn to try and get people interested, and here I just tell the simple story and God convicts them." What is the difference? One is Good *News*.

All around the world 178,000 people become Christians every single day.[6] These are overwhelming numbers. We cannot even comprehend these numbers, but God is advancing the Kingdom of Heaven into these dark regions, and people are responding in droves. Why is it often our perspective that God is not doing much? We are clawing and scratching just to get a few converts, and normally they are converts from the church down the street, or they are backsliders who were in our Sunday School years ago. We do not see God pressing forward and blowing through the gates of Hades, as He is doing on planet earth.

If you look to the horizon, you can see the dawning of that day John wrote of in Revelation, when the redeemed of every tongue, tribe and nation are gathered around the throne. I was in Mongolia, and there they explained that linguists have discovered a cultural and linguistic link between the Navajos and the Mongolians. Now there are Navajo missionaries going to Mongolia.

God is moving upon the hearts of Latin America's Christians not only to be the recipients of the blessing but also to allow God to bless others through them. In an unprecedented way, Latin American young people are feeling the call to go as missionaries. I was preaching in a small church in the obscure village of San Francisco, Mexico just south of Monterrey. At the first opportunity to respond to a missionary call, around 50% of their young people went forward, dedicating themselves to God's global cause. Many Latin Americans are going to the Muslim peoples of North Africa.

There are Chinese missionaries going to Tibet. There are Koreans going to Kazakhstan. It is an awesome time to live! What is so great about it is that no agency is going to receive credit. No one will say, "The Americans did it!" Jesus Christ alone will get the glory, as He orchestrates His Church from all over the world to finish the job of reaching every tongue, tribe and nation on planet earth.

Amazing Jesus

> Now when Jesus had entered Capernaum, a centurion came to Him, pleading with Him, saying, Lord, my servant is lying at home paralyzed, dreadfully tormented. And Jesus said to him, I will come and heal him. The centurion answered and said, Lord, I am not worthy that You should come under my roof. But only speak a word, and my servant will be healed. For I also am a man under authority, having soldiers under me. And I say to this one, Go, and he goes; and to another, Come, and he comes;

and to my servant, Do this, and he does it. When Jesus heard it,
He marveled, and said to those who followed, Assuredly, I say
to you, I have not found such great faith, not even in Israel! And
I say to you that many will come from east and west, and sit
down with Abraham, Isaac and Jacob in the kingdom of heaven
(Matt. 8: 5-11).

These Romans were supposed to be the bad guys, yet Jesus turned to the Jews
gathered around and said, *"This guy has more faith than any of you — more
than anyone I've met so far in Israel."* Rome was occupying Israel with troops
and Roman culture, customs and religion. Israel was sure that the Messiah would
come and throw off the yoke of oppression, and yet here was Jesus getting cozy
with this uncircumcised, oppressing Gentile! It was not just limited to talking;
Jesus offered to go to the Roman's unclean house and minister to his slave! Then
to make matters worse He decided to proclaim that this Roman oppressor could
teach the Jews a thing or two about faith.

Jesus marveled at the man's faith. I do not know what the expression was on His
face, whether or not His mouth dropped open. Maybe He could not contain a
really broad and surprised smile. Whatever the reaction, Jesus was astonished at
the man's faith! Someday I want to amaze Jesus. Have you ever had that ambition?
I want to have such faith in Him that I marvel Him.

There was another time that Jesus was amazed. Remember? He was in His
hometown, and He marveled that He could not do many miracles there, because
of their lack of faith. That is probably the marveling that Jesus is most familiar
with regarding our life. He marvels that He cannot do much with us, because of
our lack of faith. Just once, wouldn't you like to marvel Jesus like the Roman
Centurion did? Wouldn't it be great if your church was a church that marvels the
heart of God, because of the faith it displayed? Wouldn't it be great if you amazed
Jesus by the abandonment with which you serve Him? To marvel God is worth
being zealous.

This Roman Centurion amazed God with his humble and honest faith. "And I
say to you that many will come from the east and west" (vs. 11). Jesus was trying
to give the Jews here a little lesson in His heart for all peoples. This Roman has
the greatest faith, "And many like him will come from the east and west and will
recline at the table with Abraham, Isaac and Jacob in the Kingdom of Heaven"
(Matt. 8:11).

The Scriptures refer to God as "The God of Abraham, Isaac and Jacob." Why these
three? Why not include some other, more noteworthy individuals like Moses, or
Joseph or Samuel? God called Abraham to be a blessing to all peoples, and yet in
his first "missionary adventure," he lied about his wife, ended up getting his visa

15

revoked, and he was kicked out of the country. Jacob was known as the Deceiver, yet God wants to be identified with him? It is never the God of Abraham, Isaac, Jacob, Joseph and Moses. Why not? Because the deal was signed between God and these three in person. These three heard the covenant stated to them directly from God.

Every time Jesus referred to the God of Abraham, Isaac and Jacob, it was a reminder to the children of Israel. These were the people with whom God made that covenant: "I will bless you, and through you all nations will be blessed." This Great Covenant is repeated many times: in Genesis 18:18, 22:17-18, and then to Isaac in Genesis 26:24, and to Jacob in Genesis 28:12-14 and many more places.

Jesus turned to the crowd and reminded them that the Kingdom of Heaven was meant for such as this Roman officer. The covenant was not just about God blessing Israel; rather He emphasized that it is for all nations. From the east and the west, they will all come to this feast of God.

Father Abraham
The Bible is more than a collection of sixty-six individual books. It is correct to look at the Bible as one book. Genesis 1-11 is the introduction of the Bible. It sets the stage. You can essentially walk out of Genesis 11 into today's world and understand everything. These chapters tell us from where animals came, how we got the stars, the grass, the earth, how man and woman came to be, where sin came from, where murder started, the beginning of hunting and agriculture, the first cities, and how we came to have so many nations and languages. You could walk out of Genesis 11 and understand all you need to know about the world.

In Genesis chapter 12, God calls Abram (later on renamed Abraham), one man. God always intends to carry out His vast, eternal, global salvation plans through one man, one woman — simple people like you and me who are obedient to Him. Rather than giving up on the rest of humankind, with the selection of Abraham, God formed a beachhead. It was the beginning of His military campaign to retake the peoples of the world. Through this one man, Abraham, God promised to bless all the families on earth:

> Now the Lord said to Abram, "Go forth from your country, and from your relatives and from your father's house, to the land which I will show you; and I will make you a great nation, and I will bless you, and make your name great; and so you shall be a blessing; and I will bless those who bless you, and the one who curses you I will curse. And in you all the families of the earth shall be blessed." Gen. 12:1-3

Notice first to what God calls Abram. It was not just to geography, but to Himself. God did not say, *"There's the Promised Land over there; just take Route 66 and keep going. Then turn left . . .."* He basically said, *"Follow me."* Here is the maxim for our life. I know some people, who feel like God is calling them to be missionaries, but they do not know exactly where or they are waiting until they get a spouse. They are waiting for something that God has not yet revealed. Instead of being obedient and taking the first step they know, they are waiting for the entire picture to come together clearly. God does not work like that. As Dawson Trotman, founder of the Navigators, said, "If you cannot see very far, go as far as you can see."[7] God calls us to follow Him, to rely upon His guidance each step of the way.

The amazing thing about this calling of Abraham is its universality. All families are included in this blessing. Abraham is that proverbial stone that you throw into a pond, and the ripples spread out to the very edges.[8] It is not going to stop until it gets to the very edges. God is not some little parochial, tribal deity. It was not that He was going to bless Israel and zap all of their enemies. He is the God of all, and His concern is for all.

In AD 423, a monk named Simon left his monastery to live on pillars. He kept building taller and taller ones; the last was sixty feet high and four feet across. He lived there for the last thirty-five years of his life. Though we consider his action extreme, many in the Church are likewise comfortably removing themselves from the needs of mankind. Our God desires us to be channels of blessing. That is why He not only promised to bless Abraham, but also through him all nations were to be blessed. In a time when many alarmist Christian voices are calling for food stockpiles and remote communities, we are called to take His blessing to the world. Jesus echoes this anti-isolationist mentality: "I do not pray that You should take them out of the world, but that You should keep them from the evil one" (John 17:15).

God even changed Abram's name to Abraham. Abraham means "The Father of many nations." If Abraham were only about Israel, God would have called him "Father of the nation I love." It has always been about "many nations." God changed Sarai to Sarah, "Mother of kings and princes of nations."

Blessings from Heaven

Exactly what is this "blessing?" Is it cars? Is it money? Does God want to bless you with a swimming pool? Doubtful. Though "blessing" has some manifestation in the physical realm, it means far beyond that. "Blessing" is an ambiguous word. What does it mean when we say, "Bless you"? We are not always sure what a blessing is. We know it is good stuff, but it goes a little deeper than that. The word "bless" is the Hebrew word *barak*, which can be translated "bless" or "relationship."[8] God says, "I will bless you and through you all nations will be blessed." Replace the word "bless" with the other optional word, "relationship": *"I will be in relationship with you, and through you all nations will have this relationship extended to them."* That sounds a little more New Testament, doesn't it? God will bring us into right relationship with Him, and through us, He desires to extend this *barak*, this blessing of right relationship, to the nations. The New Testament authors also interpreted this:

> You are sons of the prophets, and of the covenant which God made with our fathers, saying to Abraham, And in your seed all the families of the earth shall be blessed. To you first, God, having raised up His Servant Jesus, sent Him **to bless you, in turning away every one of you from your iniquities** (Acts 3:25-26).

Paul, in chapter 3 of Galatians talks about the blessing being righteousness. This is essential, turning from sin and receiving His righteousness, so that we may be in relationship with God.

Promise Fulfilled

In Genesis 12, God is establishing a thesis. Maybe you remember those bluebook essays in school. First, you had to establish your purpose, or your thesis statement, at the top — "This is what I plan to prove in my essay" stated right there at the beginning. Then throughout the rest of the essay, you try to fill in the details of your thesis. This is what God did here in Genesis 12. He called Abram, later Abraham, and He said, *"I will bless you and through you all the nations will be blessed."* This was God establishing His direction, what He is going to do through the rest of scripture and the rest of time. In Revelation, we see the completion of His plan:

> After these things I looked, and behold, a great multitude which no one could number, of all nations, tribes, peoples, and tongues, standing before the throne and before the Lamb, clothed with white robes, with palm branches in their hands (Rev. 7:9).

How many were there? It was a multitude that no one could count. John could not count how many individuals there were in front of the throne, but he could see that there were representatives from every tongue, tribe and nation. Every tongue, tribe and nation will have some of its people redeemed by the blood of the Lamb, by Jesus Christ and His sacrifice, and they will stand before the throne worshiping Him forever with us. This is going to happen. This is the conclusion of time. God is not a liar. What He established in Genesis 12, He will accomplish sometime in the future.

Geopolitical nations are different from ethnic nations. We understand that the Cherokee Nation is a nation within the country of the United States of America. In the same way, within countries that do have the church, there still are nations that have no access to the Gospel. In these nations, or peoples, there are no Christians who speak their language. No one has gone there and planted the Church. There still are such places on planet earth. Mission agencies can look across the earth and know where these unreached nations and peoples live. Imagine this! We know what we have left to do to get the Good News of Jesus Christ to every nation on planet earth! These are exciting times. We can look at the world and say, "The Good News hasn't been here yet." Well, let's go! That is where we are in history.

Do you know what the next step is in history? Revelation! Every tongue, tribe and nation clothed in righteousness, redeemed by the blood of the Lamb, finally will stand before the Father and worship. We are within striking distance of that for the first time in the history of the world. God so loves the world that He has called us to be His special people and take this right relationship with God to the ends of the earth. This was Abraham, Isaac and Jacob's commission. It is the commission of every person who is a son or daughter of Abraham. God still intends to bless us and through us bless all the peoples of the earth.

Notes

1. H. Robert Cowles, K. Neill Foster and David P. Jones, *Missionary Voices* (Camphill, Pennsylvania: Christian Publications, 1996) pp. 267-268.

2. David Wang, Praying with Power Conference, Colorado Springs, CO, February 12, 1999.

3. Bill and Amy Stearns, *Catch the Vision 2000* (Minneapolis: Bethany House Publishers, 1991) p. 16.

4. Fred Markert, Strategic Frontiers YWAM speaking at Solid Rock Church (Colorado Springs: 1997).

5. Patrick Johnstone, *The Church Is Bigger Than You Think* (Pasadena: William Carey Library, 1998) p. 115.

6. David B. Barrett and Todd M. Johnson, *Our Globe and How to Reach It* (Birmingham: New Hope, 1990) p. 32.

7. Dawson Trotman, quoted by Ralph D. Winter in "The Abrahamic Connection," USCWM, Pasadena, CA, 1995.

8. Bernard W. Anderson, *The Unfolding Drama of the Bible* (New York: Association Press, 1957) p. 18.

9. Walter Kaiser, Old Testament Survey Tape Series, Trinity Evangelical Divinity School.

four

God So Loved the World

"Some there are who speak disparagingly of the blessed
and holy work of evangelization. We tremble for them.
We feel persuaded they are not in the current of the
Master's mind, and hence we utterly reject their thoughts.
It is to be feared that their hearts are cold in reference to
an object that engages the **heart of God**."[1]
C.H. Mackintosh

"In the beginning God created the heavens and the earth."
Genesis 1:1

My version reads a little differently. It says, "In the beginning God created the heavens and *Israel*." No, it does not really say that, but isn't that how we sometimes read scripture — like God somewhere along the line lost interest in the rest of the planet and said, *"Forget them. This is the people that I'm really going to focus on"?*

If you need a missionary theology, if you need a basis for missiology, here it is: "In the beginning God created the heavens and the earth" — *the whole thing.* From the very beginning, God's activity and nature has been the whole earth. He took a chaotic mess and made order, darkness and made light, ugliness and made beauty, and He has done that in my life. He has taken ugliness, darkness and chaos and made order, light and life. From the beginning to the present, the scope of His interest and activity has always been global.

The earth is the Lord's and all it contains, the world and all those who dwell in it (Psalms 24:1).

Nation of Priests
So what was Israel's special role with God? Clearly, they were singled out for a unique and special relationship with God, but what exactly was it? Israel's

21

calling, commissioning and sole reason for existence is found in God's covenant with Abraham. (Gen. 12:2) God desired to bless all peoples through Abraham's descendants. Israel had no reason to exist, except as the bearer of an unmingled and undefiled faith in Jehovah to every nation.[2] Proclaiming the greatness of His name among the nations was their mandate for life.

God reminded the children of Abraham of this repeatedly. Even before God gave them the law on tablets, which would define Judaism and the life of Israel, God wanted to remind them of their Prime Directive:

> And you shall be to Me a kingdom of priests and a
> holy nation. (Ex. 19:6a)

We all have an idea of what a priest is. A priest represents God to the people and the people to God. A priest is a go-between. If a man is a priest, he is a priest to individuals. Here God commissioned a nation of priests, but to whom were they to be priests? Other nations. God is saying, *"You are to be a nation of priests. That is your reason for existence."* Only after clarifying once more their overarching purpose, did He finally give them the law.

The same parallel exists for the Church today. We are the new Israel. The Church has the same mandate to be a "kingdom of priests" ministering to God and to the nations. We are to extend this right relationship to every tongue, tribe and nation. Paul W. Powell correctly states:

> The church that loses its sense of mission is in peril of its life.
> The church exists by mission as a fire exists by burning. Let a
> fire cease to burn and it becomes ashes. Let the church cease
> to be missionary and evangelistic and it ceases to be a church
> — and the coldness and dullness of death sets in.[3]

If the Church only exists for right relationship with God, then when we first became Christians, God would have "beamed us up" to heaven right then. There would be no reason to be on earth. When you knelt at that altar, you were the cleanest you will ever get. If purity was the only issue, or if getting to heaven was the only issue on God's mind, we would already be there. S.D. Gordon, in 1906, wrote:

> I like greatly the motto of the Salvation Army. It must have
> been born for those workers in the warm heart of the mother of
> the Army, Catherine Booth. That mother explains much of the
> marvelous power of that organization. Their motto is, "Saved
> to Serve." Some seem to put the period in after the first word.
> That's bad punctuation and worse Christianity. We are saved to
> be savers.[4]

God has a reason for leaving us here on earth and that is for the extension of His kingdom, His blessing to every tongue, tribe and nation. This is our purpose. The Theology of Missions is the Theology of the Church. We have no reason to exist other than this. You cannot understand Israel, or the Church and God's dealings with us without comprehending our missionary intent and mandate.

Somehow, the Church has successfully ignored her purpose for being left on earth. Robert Glover, over fifty years ago, wrote:

> Alas that the Church has to so large an extent lost its original missionary vision, has not kept its eye on the circumference of the circle, "the uttermost part of the earth"! In the measure in which it has ceased pressing on and out to the whole world, the Lord's blessing has been withheld, and the miracle of His wonder-working power and increase has ceased. One hears of this and that church being financially embarrassed and not being able to make ends meet. We venture to say that on investigation it will be found that those churches have lost, or have never had, the evangelistic and missionary vision and outreach. How can any church claim or expect the Lord's blessing while neglecting the very object for which it was created? What interest has God in helping any church "make ends meet" merely around itself? We have yet to see a truly missionary church struggling for its own financial support. It still remains true that when the Lord's people "seek first the kingdom of God," all these necessary things will be added unto them.

> "Where there is no vision, the people perish." Think of the awful fact that nineteen hundred years after Jesus Christ died on the Cross "for the sins of the whole world," hundreds of millions are still living and dying without ever having been told a word about it! Think of those vast solid areas — where the task of evangelization has not merely to be finished, but has at this late date yet to be begun! Think of a thousand tribal languages into which not a word of the God who so loves the world has yet been translated! Nor have the existing missionary forces more than barely touched the fringe of the total need in field after field that we call "occupied." The huge proportions of the unfinished task of missions even in this advanced day are nothing less than staggering, and how anyone who has experienced the blessings of Christ's salvation can view the situation without deep conviction and concern is beyond our understanding.[5]

Who Do Ya Love?

There is some confusion in the North American Evangelical mind regarding Israel. When it comes to the modern state of Israel and the Arab nations, we feel as though we are betraying God if we sympathize with the plight of the Palestinians. There is something latent in all of us Sunday School pupils that thinks the Palestinians are like those rascal Philistines of old . . . and didn't God hate them?

> Well did He? Let's take a quick quiz. Whom does God love more?
> > The Israelites or those rascal Philistines?
> > The Israelites or the Arameans?
> > The Israelites or the Ethiopians?

> "Are you not as the sons of Ethiopia to me, O sons of Israel?" declares the Lord. "Have I not brought up Israel out of the land of Egypt, and the Philistines from Caphtor and the Arameans from Kir?" (Amos 9:7)

> If you did not do so well, here is your chance to redeem yourself:
> Who are God's people?
> > The Egyptians
> > The Assyrians
> > The Israelites

> Blessed is Egypt, My people, and Assyria, the work of My hands, and Israel, my inheritance (Is. 19:25).

How did you do? We mistakenly think that God, in choosing Israel, was rejecting the rest of His peoples. The truth is that He has been working for their salvation all along, revealing Himself, wooing them, and preparing through Abraham's seed the avenue for reconciliation.

Levites and Israelites

The dynamic tension between *I have chosen you from among all the peoples to be a special treasure,* and *all the peoples of the world belong to God,* can be resolved quite simply by a third quiz. Whom did God love more?
> The Levites or the Benjamites?
> The Levites or the Reubenites?
> The Levites or the Gadites?

Did you do better this time? God's love is for all, however the Levites had a special task to fulfill unto God and the other tribes. They were to be priests to the tribes of Israel. So also Abraham's children had a special calling to Him, in purity of walk and devotion of their whole heart, and in their priestly duties to the tribes, tongues and nations of the earth. *(For further study compare Deut. 7:6 with Deut. 18:5.)*

This brings us to you and me. Since the reformation was founded on this basic principle of the universal priesthood of the believers, I trust that I will receive no argument. Through Christ, the way has been paved for us not only to approach the throne directly, but also through Christ we have received the commission to minister to men. Paul taught this, and John in Revelation saw it clearly:

> Worthy art thou . . . for with thy blood you purchased men from every tribe and tongue and people and nation. And thou hast made them to be a kingdom and priests to our God and they will reign upon the earth! (Rev. 5:9-10)

What a powerful vision of the Church of Jesus Christ. We are His purchased priests and kingdom rulers on earth. This is the high calling of all that are in Christ — to be His priests on earth, and as Israel was responsible for the spiritual well being of the nations, so are we.

As priests, we have an important message to convey: "In the past God allowed the peoples to go their own way, but now He is declaring to men everywhere that they should repent because He has fixed a day for judgement!" (Acts 17:30-31)

God's Preparation

It may seem unfair on God's part to let the peoples wander and now demand that they repent. However, their wandering was not the same as getting lost. It was more like running away from home. Like prodigals, the nations turned their backs on the knowledge of God and became foolish and dark in their thinking. (Rom. 1:21) The result of their wandering can be seen all about us, in the idolatry of Asia and the licentiousness of the West.

I was walking with a new friend of mine in Taiwan through one of the island's oldest temples. He lit an incense stick and began to pray to the idol sitting before him on the altar. Almost absentmindedly, he asked me if I would desire to pray to his god. I responded perhaps a bit too forcefully, "No, I worship the one true God, the Maker of heaven and the earth!"

Without a blink he answered, "Yes, we know of Him, but we cannot reach Him. He is far away, so we worship the gods at hand."

Several years later, I was in the mountains of Taiwan at a Hakka wedding. There were no Christians in the family, in fact there were few Christians in the entire people group at the time. As I was observing the marriage ceremony, a friend of mine explained each step. The woman of the house bowed low before her gods on their shelf to pray that all would go well with the ceremony and then stepped to the threshold of her door. With a trinity of bows toward heaven, she placed three incense sticks in a holder by the door. My friend turned to me and exclaimed, "That was to your God."

The sad truth is that all peoples on planet earth knew of the Creator God but have lost much of their knowledge. Many of them know of His existence, yet understand somehow that there is a block to communication. This is a perfect picture of sin. Jesus became the bridge to span this chasm of sin between men on one side and God on the other. Now is the time He is sending us, His priests, to tell the nations of His provision, salvation and reconciliation, and to call them to repentance.

I spent some time with His priests in northern Thailand. I will never forget the lessons God taught me, as I served with these pioneer missionaries who were daily risking it all for the Gospel. While there I spent some time with a unique, tribal people named the Karen.

The Karen believe that, as a people, they were the oldest son of God. God had seven sons. The next was the Burmese, then the Chinese, etc. They believe that the white brother was the youngest. The Karen are a slash and burn culture, and one day while they were out clearing their field, God came and said He was going on a long trip across the ocean. He asked if the Karen would like to go with Him. The Karen told Him that he was too busy. God asked each of the brothers, but they all declined to go, except the youngest brother, the white brother. God and the white brother went far away across the sea.

When they got to their destination, God wrote a book and sent it back to the Karen to tell him how to get to where God was. When Karen received it, he was still busy clearing his field, so he put it on a stump. Forgetting it was there, he burned the field and lost the book. Ever since, the Karen people have mourned the loss of the book. They also had a story that foretold that one day their white brother would return from across the sea and sit under a tree with a book and tell them how to get to God.

One day, a missionary stepped out of a boat and sat down under a tree with his Bible. The rest of the story is that many of the Karen have become Christians. God was preparing them, and they were ready to receive the Good News when it arrived.

This should thrill your soul, as you see not only a God who calls them to repent, but also prepares them to receive Him. The missionary task is not to take Jesus there, but to be obedient, as He takes us there to minister among His people. May we be His faithful priests, as He establishes His kingdom on earth in the hearts of people from every tongue, tribe and nation.

> You will be called the priests of the Lord; You will be spoken of as ministers of our God; You will eat the wealth of nations And in their glory you will boast . . . The Spirit of the Lord is upon me, Because the Lord has anointed me To bring good news to the afflicted. He has sent me to bind up the brokenhearted To proclaim liberty to the captives And freedom to prisoners To proclaim the favorable year of the Lord And the day of vengeance of our God . . .
> (from Isaiah 61)

Notes
1. C.H. Mackintosh, *The Great Commission, Miscellaneous Writings, Volume IV* (New York: Loizeaux Brothers, 1898), p. GC-87.
2. J.H. Bavink, *An Introduction to the Science of Missions* (Philadelphia, PA: The Presbyterian and Reformed Publishing Co., 1960), p. 18.
3. Paul W. Powell, *The Church Today* (Annuity Board of the Southern Baptist Convention, 1997), p. 19.
4. S. D. Gordon, *Quiet Talks On Service* (New York: Fleming H. Revell Company, 1906), p. 118.
5. Robert Hall Glover, *The Bible Basis of Missions* (Los Angeles, CA: Bible House of Los Angeles, 1946), pp. 193-194.

five

No Other Name

"The missionary enterprise is no human conception or
undertaking, no modern scheme or invention . . . It did not
originate in the brain or heart of any man, not even
William Carey, or the Apostle Paul. Its source was in the
heart of God Himself. And Jesus Christ, God's great
Missionary to a lost world, was the supreme revelation of
His heart and expression of His love."[1]
Robert Hall Glover

A Prostitute's Confession

Now before they lay down, she came up to them on
the roof, and said to the men: I know that the Lord
has given you the land, that the terror of you has
fallen on us, and that all the inhabitants of the land
are fainthearted because of you. For we have heard
how the Lord dried up the water of the Red Sea for
you when you came out of Egypt, and what you did to
the two kings of the Amorites who were on the other
side of the Jordan, Sihon and Og, whom you utterly
destroyed. And as soon as we heard these things,
our hearts melted; neither did there remain anymore
courage in anyone because of you, for the Lord your
God, He is God in heaven above and on earth beneath
(Josh. 2:8-11).\

As we read of Rahab, the prostitute, spilling all this out on the spies, the question
arises, "How does she know all this?" Jericho had no *CNN Headline News*, yet
somehow she knew all about what had happened to Sihon and Og. From any
military analysis, it should not have happened — a rag-tag band of refugees in
the desert with no defensive posture available destroys these two kingdoms and

their kings. It was a supernatural event, that no one could explain away, and that testimony exalted God.

You may be tempted to say, "It's such brutality." Before you succumb, notice what it did to the surrounding nations. They all saw that this event was not "normal." It was supranormal — supernatural. When the people of Israel gave credit to their God, the surrounding nations wondered, "Maybe it is true. Perhaps their God is different."

Every day the people of Israel were guarded by a pillar of fire by night, and they followed a supernatural cloud by day. Imagine the tense conversations in Jericho as the cloud loomed on the horizon:

> "What is that? Is there a thunderstorm coming our way?"
> "I don't think so. It's been there for three days now."
> "Is it coming closer?"
> "Yeah, it's coming closer."
> "Do you know what it is?"
> "Well I heard a rumor that this is the same thing that Sihon and Og saw before Israel showed up on their doorstep."

Have you ever been out in the desert in the night? You can see the stars so clearly, because there are no city lights interfering. A campfire out in the desert lights up the whole sky and reflects off canyon walls for miles. The fire that guarded the Israelites was no little campfire. It was big enough to stop all of Pharaoh's army at the Red Sea. It probably lit up the sky like a forest fire. Imagine Jericho. Every night the fire glow was a little bit closer. This explains why the spies were discovered so quickly in Jericho. Jericho was on red alert! With millions of people and a campfire from heaven, Israel had trouble sneaking up on anybody.

Jericho was terrified. Rahab confessed that. No man had any courage left in him. Of what were they terrified? Was it Israel's strength, their army? It was their God. The Israelite's God had proven Himself supernatural. Even this prostitute knew that He was not some idol; He was **God**. What a great testimony!

We need to learn an important principle from this testimony: *Many of God's miraculous deeds had the immediate purpose of saving Israel, but the ultimate purpose of making God's name known to the nations.* God wanted to be known, and He was building a reputation through His obedient servant, Israel. It was not for Israel's sake alone that He saved their neck, but so that the surrounding nations would wake up and see Him as God!

> Look to me, and be saved, all the ends of the earth! For I am God and there is no other (Is. 45:22).

Supernatural Testimony

Just as the fire of God was a supernatural testimony to the surrounding nations, so also were the unlikely victories of the rag-tag Israelites over the superior armies like Sihon and Og. Remember Joshua fighting down in the valley while Moses was up on the hill "winning it" for them? This was not a natural battle. The physical fact is that their enemies should have ruled the day. But we are not worshiping a God who has to play by the rules of "might makes right." Moses went up on the hill. As long as he kept his hands raised, the "undergunned" army won. When he tired, the natural, rough and tumble military flexed its muscle. Israel fought this battle on two levels, the physical and the spiritual.

Time even stood still for one battle. News of the victory traveled far and wide: The Day the Sun Stood Still and Those Who Should Have Lost Won. God is in the business of supernatural interventions and activity that the world might know He is God.

> In mainland China, a certain Christian worked in the office that controlled all the electrical power used in a large, underground mining operation where four hundred miners labored deep in the earth.
>
> One day this Christian felt the strong urge to pull the alarm switch, which would bring the entire mining operation to a halt and call the miners to the surface.
>
> Naturally, he did his best to resist the inclination because he had no rational basis for the urge to pull the alarm. What would his supervisor say if he shut down the entire mine for no good reason? But he could not escape the feeling that he had to sound a general alarm.
>
> At last he put his hand on the alarm switch — and pulled. Sirens moaned and red lights began to flash deep in the mineshafts. Four hundred miners hurried to the surface. Supervisors poured into the office angrily asking what had gone wrong. Several top managers surrounded the man who had sounded the alarm, demanding to know why he had done it.
>
> Just at that moment, there was a terrifying roar, the earth shook, and the entire mine collapsed. When everyone had recovered from the initial shock, they asked: "How did you know the mine was going to collapse?"
>
> "My God told me to pull the switch," was the reply.

"If your God can do that, he must be worth knowing," was the general response. Today that man is the pastor of an underground church with four hundred members.[2]

No Other Name

Our God lives to show Himself strong on behalf of His people, so as to exalt His name above all other deities and idols. Why does God want to exalt His Name above every other name? Is it because He is an egotist? No! *It is because there is no other name by which man can be saved.* If they do not know His Name, they do not know His salvation. If He does not exalt His Name above common idols made of stone and wood, how will anyone know whom to call upon in their day of need? How will any true seeker find his way to our God?

The Nations are the Focus

> Therefore say to the house of Israel, "Thus says the Lord God: "I do not do this for your sake, O house of Israel, but for My holy name's sake, which you have profaned among the nations wherever you went. And I will sanctify my great name, which has been profaned among the nations, which you have profaned in their midst; and the nations shall know that I am the Lord," says the Lord God, "when I am hallowed in you before their eyes" (Ez. 36:22-24).

The world is the focus here. This was the reason for God's sending them into captivity, and this is the reason that He was going to rescue them. God says, *"My reputation has gone down the tubes because of you guys, so I'm going to do something. It's not because you guys deserve it, but I am going to do this, so that My Name is exalted among the nations."* Why? Because there is no other name under heaven by which men might be saved. If His Name is profaned, they are definitely not going to turn to Him. They will think that He is just like every other god. God was concerned about His reputation, for the sake of the nations. (Ez. 15:6-8)

God is in the business of building His reputation. Sadly, His people who are to build up God's reputation in the eyes of a doubting world are often faithless, bringing shame to His Name. His intent is for those of us called by His great Name to put ourselves in situations for Him to glorify His Name through us.

> Tommy Titcombe of the Sudan Interior Mission has described a time when he was working among the Yagba tribe. A long dry spell hit the area. The pagans of the community made sacrifices and prayed a whole week for rain. After that the Moslems prayed for a week with no success. Then in the Sunday church service of the Christians the pastor turned to Titcombe and said,

"White man, isn't it time for us who belong to the Lord Jesus to pray for rain?"

The next evening the congregation held a special meeting to pray for rain, and they expected it right away. The aisles of the church were filled with the cumbersome rain hats worn by these people.

Titcombe asked, "What are you doing with those things in the church?"

They replied, "Oh, white man, haven't we come to pray for rain? We'll need those when we go out."

The animists were looking in from one side of the church and the Moslems from another. It was a clear, starlit night without a cloud in the sky. The Christians got down on their knees, and within half an hour God had sent them a tremendous downpour.

Praise the Lord for his mighty acts among the children of men...[3]

God, even our God, will glorify Himself in the eyes of the nations so that they might know there is none that compare!

Notes
1. Robert Hall Glover, *The Bible Basis of Missions* (Los Angeles, CA: Bible House of Los Angeles, 1946), p. 13.
2. Richard R. DeRidder and Roger S. Greenway, *Let the Whole World Know* (Grand Rapids, MI: Baker Book House, 1988), p. 108-109.
3. David Brainerd Woodward, (Gospel Light Publications, 1964), p. 114-115.

six

High Drama

"Can anything exceed this in interest? Who can fail to see
in the fact here recorded that it was the loving desire of
the **heart of God** to reach every creature under heaven
with the sweet story of His grace?"[1]
C.H. Mackintosh

The thought of trying to write a brief book on God's heart for the world is terrifying, if not impossible. I feel somewhat like the American tourist that I encountered one summer in Paris. I was an art student, "living" the better part of a week in the Louvre, and she was rushing through, as though she would establish a new track record of "been there, done that." This material will hopefully not inoculate you from further learning, but rather, spur you on to your own deeper study.

We Saw the Movie
With the release of the *Prince of Egypt* on the big screen, a new generation was introduced to the story of God's saving Israel through Moses. Much like its predecessor, *The Ten Commandments*, it graphically details the plagues that brought Egypt to her knees. The plagues effectively forced Pharaoh to "let My people go." However, was that the whole reason? Was God just trying to wrestle His people free? Let's see:

> For at this time I will send all My plagues to your very heart, and
> on your servants and on your people, **that you may know that
> there is none like Me in all the earth.** Now if I had stretched
> out My hand and struck you and your people with pestilence,
> then you would have been cut off from the earth. But indeed for
> this purpose I have raised you up, **that I may show My power
> in you, and that My name may be declared in all the earth**
> (Ex. 9:14-16).

35

High Drama

God in His great love for the Egyptians was giving them time to repent. He said, *"By now I could have just wiped you off the face of the earth, but I didn't."* Why didn't God just put His finger on the smite button and zap all the Egyptians? He could have, but chose not to. Scripture says that He wanted to show the Egyptians that He is God. He was concerned for the Egyptians. If the plagues had been only for Israel's sake, God could have just "smitten" the Egyptians for them.

Sometimes when I consider the story of how the Israelites were finally released, I wonder what all the "game playing" was about. If God wanted to get His people free, why not just play the trump card from the beginning? Did God have to get out His miracle machine and dust it off? Was it like He said, *"I've only got enough power for little miracles. Do the leprosy thing in your shirt. Pull it out . . . Put it back in . . . Now, do the snake thing, Moses"*? Moses threw his rod down and voila . . . a snake. All the court magicians promptly did the same thing. Okay, so our snake did eat all of theirs, but it was hardly convincing, somewhere more along the lines of parlor tricks. Perhaps the miracle-o-meter was not charged up enough. (The longer it is plugged in, the more power available for the "bigger" type plagues.) *"At about 6 bazillian watts (bzw) we'll go for blood in their water, at 7 bzw's — frogs, 8 bzw's — the flies."*

The plagues were more than just a power demonstration; they were specifically targeted to bring the Egyptians to the saving knowledge of God. Each one of the nine plagues was a direct challenge to the gods of Egypt. One by one, God showed His might as superior to the local deities: Ha'pi the god of the Nile, Heqit who was symbolized by frogs; God darkened the sun proving His power over Ra, the sun god. In His final demonstration of superiority over the Egyptian gods, the great I AM defeated the power of the god-king Pharaoh by taking his firstborn son.[2]

> For I will pass through the land of Egypt on that night, and will strike all the firstborn in the land of Egypt, both man and beast; and *against all the gods of Egypt* I will execute judgement: I am the Lord (Ex. 12:12).

Pharaoh and his people were being introduced to the God above all others. At the beginning of this encounter Pharaoh said, "Who is the Lord that I should obey His voice? I do not know the Lord." (Ex. 5:2) God could have just wiped out the Egyptians, but He gave them mercy. He wanted them to know Him and be blessed with this right relationship. God's efforts proved fruitful. After the firstborn son of every Egyptian family died and the Hebrews began to leave Egypt, many Egyptians went out with them to worship the one, true God. Egypt also piled high the Children of Abraham with gifts of jewels and livestock. God was effective in His testimony unto Himself, exalting Himself above the common deities.

The Exodus was not all about Israel. Though it had the immediate effect of saving

Israel, it had the ultimate purpose of making God's Name exalted in all the earth. He was exalted among the Egyptians and all the other nations that heard the story. Powerful God. Merciful God.

Master Thespian
God, through the plagues, focused the attention of the world on the events in Egypt. He riveted the attention of every Hebrew and Egyptian. With each call to let My people go, and the corresponding defiance, came a pause where everyone waited to see what would happen. There is a tangible tension in the air when a dramatic pause is effective. The whole world seems to stop, while all eyes focus on the unfolding drama. What will happen? Will the good guys survive? I think that all of heaven had a dramatic pause when Abraham in obedience raised his knife-clutched hand over the young body of his and Heaven's dear, loved child of promise. At the last second, God ordered an angel to the rescue.

God seems to know how to use these dramatic episodes to focus the eyes of the world on His children, Israel. Over and over again, we see impossible odds overcome, last minute rescues, and His chosen people set on their feet in safety. The famous director of films, Cecil B. DeMille, once said, "The greatest source of material for motion pictures is the Bible, and almost any chapter in the Bible would serve as a basic idea for a motion picture."[3]

The God of the Last Minute
What is the rush, if a day is like a thousand years to God? Our last minute is like 252 days in which He has to work things out. Our God does have things under control. We often just wish He would reveal His plans a bit sooner.

I remember banging my head against the steering wheel of my car in hopelessness. I groaned to my wife, "We will never get the money we need in time!" We had sent out letters to everyone we knew, and still we were over a thousand dollars short of the ticket purchase price, and the deadline was barely a week away. My faith was not that of the Roman Centurion's. We had been living without any visible means of support for several years, and God had never let us down, always providing for our needs. But this was different. We felt that He was calling us to take a team of others on a "Joshua Walk" (a prayer walk) through Taiwan. We were the leaders and could not find the money. All our sources were tapped out.

I turned to my wife, "Maybe we didn't hear right. Perhaps only I was to go, and you were to stay." In quick response, she got out her notes from her time with the Lord that morning. She said, "I asked the Lord again if we were messed up or if He really wanted us both to go, and as loud as you are talking to me, He said, *"Sit back and watch the show."* I did not know if I could believe it or not. After all, it was just one week (Let's see, that would be 7,000 years for Him to try and work something out.). But the show did start.

After church the next day, a friend came up and handed me $400. Then someone donated a "hot-rod" to us. That was nice, but it was money we needed at the moment — not a car. The donor had said if we could sell it, we could use the money, so we put an ad in the paper and parked the car in front of my father-in-law's house. Five days to go and counting. The morning the money was due, I was pacing. The doorbell rang, and there stood my father-in-law with $1,100 cash in his hand. The car had sold. J. Hudson Taylor said over a hundred years ago, "God's work done in God's way will not lack God's supply."[4]

Our God is the *God of the last minute rescue*, but will we be willing to be *people of the last minute rescue*? Will we rest for His salvation or will we bail out on Him? God wants to set up those watching for that dramatic pause. Then, only He can rescue. Will we wait, or will we grab ourselves off the altar, forgetting that He desires to dramatically display His love and provision for us through this momentary crisis. Remember, the Children of Israel always seemed to lose sight of this reality. Will we?

Why the Red Sea Split

> For the Lord your God dried up the waters of the Jordan before you until you had crossed over, as the Lord your God did to the Red Sea, which He dried up before us until we had crossed over, **that all the peoples of the earth may know the hand of the Lord, that it is mighty, that you may fear the Lord your God forever** (Josh. 4:23-24).

In this passage, the reason that God let them pass through the Red Sea and the Jordan is clearly stated. It was not simply so that they could get safely to the other side. There was a much greater purpose than that. Maybe when God rescued them from Egypt, He just had not gone that way before. Maybe He did not know the direct route to the Promised Land.

Have you seen those chase scenes in the movies where the character ducks down an alley, around a corner and invariably runs into a dead end? Just as he realizes his predicament, the pursuers arrive, cutting off any means of escape. I think Israel felt just like that when they saw the cloud of dust coming.

Maybe God said, *"Wow. When did I put this sea here?"* Before He had time to decide what to do, He turned and saw the chariots of Pharaoh bearing down on the slave escapees. He dusted off His miracle-o-meter and plugged it in again. When the power was adequate, He said, *"Okay, wall of fire!"* Boom! The Egyptians stopped, and the children of Israel were freaking out. The miracle-o-meter geared up a little more, and suddenly there was enough power to make a path through the water. The children of Israel got across, and the miracle-o-meter, due to all the energy that it was expending because of this giant miracle, shorted out, collapsing the Red Sea on the Egyptians.

Though that is not what happened, somehow in the back of our mind, we think that God made a mistake getting them there. No. It was not for Israel's sake that He led them to the Red Sea. If He had been singly concerned about Israel and their safety, He would have guided them directly to begin with. He could have even teleported them like He did Philip in the New Testament — suddenly they would find themselves in the Promised Land saying, "Cool. How did we get here?" Our God is not so weak that He cannot do things like that. Opening the Red Sea is not any less of a miracle than teleporting them into the Promised Land, but He purposely led them to a dead end, so that all the peoples of the earth might know of His might.

The Israelites were thinking that they were going to die for sure. Sometimes we find ourselves in a similar situation. We have no escape possible. Our back is to the Red Sea. The Egyptians are coming down on us, and this is it. Again, God does it for His Name's
sake, that we might fear Him, that we might have a revelation that He is God, as Israel did when they crossed the Red Sea. They had a worship party like few have seen when they got to the other side.

Jamie's Finger
The other reason God waits until the last minute is so that the nations, when they hear about the power of God, will be amazed. My wife is a great pianist. I love to hear her playing, worshiping God by just playing for no audience other than Jesus. She has used her gift to lead others in worship. One day after the Sunday service, she came to me rubbing her hand. At the base of her finger, a bump had formed. We watched it for several weeks hoping it would just go away (You know, the ol' "head in the sand" routine.). Finally the pain was so intense that she could no longer play the piano. We went to a doctor in the church. He examined it and pronounced the bad news. It was a ganglion that was attached to the tendon of the finger. There was only one cure and that was surgery. However, Jamie's finger may have been permanently damaged after its removal.

This was not good news. We prayed about it and felt that God was telling us to wait, that He would heal it. We told the doctor of our decision, and he frowned a bit but said nothing. Periodically, he would see us at church and ask how it was. For a couple of months there was no change, but we continued to pray and hold on to what God had said. Then one day the doctor asked about the bump. Jamie felt where the bump should have been, but it was gone! His mouth dropped open, and we all began to cry as we rejoiced in the healing that God had provided. Jamie's life was on display for the faith of our doctor friend. God could have healed it the first time we prayed, but in His perfect timing He was creating a dramatic pause to capture the attention of this doctor.

In Scripture, God used this drama of last minutes, dead ends and path-clearing to really "wow" the nations. As far as the story of the Exodus was told, people said, "That God of Israel is not a normal God. He is supernatural. He is God." But in His great love He does not leave it in the realm of only entertainment. He challenges our paradigms and demands our response, interaction and involvement. It is not a TV show; it is a part of the drama of our real life. Paul Minear puts it this way:

> It is as if in the theater, where I am hugely enjoying an esthetic view of life, God interrupts the show with a *[thundering]* announcement: "Is John Smith in the house?" And I am John Smith. And the interruption continues: "Report immediately . . . for a task intended for you alone."[5]

God does not allow the nations and the peoples just to watch the drama, but gets them involved, through a direct encounter or the general challenge issued to their idols, *"I am God and there is no other!"*

And with us, His people, He asks us to get involved. I remember, my dad used to preach a sermon that went along these lines, "There are two kinds of people in the world: those who are in the football game and those who are in the stands. The first group is involved, while the second just watches . . .." I doubt this does the sermon justice, but the message struck home with me. God is issuing the challenge to us to be involved in this unfolding drama of His. He desires us to be willing actors in His display of power and love before the lost of the earth. (1 Cor. 4:9) He wants us to become part of the cast that **declares** His marvelous deeds among the nations, His mercy that is available to all that ask. (Ps. 96:3)

> The Greek word for **declare** comes from the Greek theater. Imagine a large audience watching drama. Much has happened on stage, but as the scene is changed, a messenger enters the stage to "declare" to the audience what is taking place "behind the scenes," off-stage, concealed from the view of the audience. His information helps them understand the action of the people on-stage.

> Peter says that God made us, His church, a chosen people, so that we can be the messengers who come to the center stage of the world and tell the spectators what God is doing "behind the scenes," even though they do not know about Him and cannot understand what he is doing in our world. The world will come to know Him only if we tell them.[6]

So much of our Bible has been interpreted as having been for our benefit only or for the children of Israel's benefit. Never did we realize that God wanted to display His greatness and salvation power to the nations through Israel. These are some of our favorite Sunday School stories, yet somehow we are largely unaware of God's love and activity for the nations. All we see is God's desire for Israel. Getting Israel out of Egypt was all about saving Israel's neck, right? Wrong! It had to do with God's making His Name known among the nations. Israel was just His chosen player to reveal that truth.

> The Lord has bared His holy arm in the sight of all the nations,
> that all the ends of the earth may see the salvation of our God
> (Is. 52:10).

Notes

1. C.H. Mackintosh, *The Great Commission, Miscellaneous Writings, Volume IV,* (New York: Loizeaux Brothers, 1898) p. GC-91.
2. Dr. David Burnett, *God's Mission: Healing the Nations* (Send the Light Books, 1984), p. 64.
3. Frank S. Mead, *Encyclopedia of Religious Quotations* (London: Peter Davies Ltd., 1965), p. 26.
4. Vinita Hampton and Carol Plueddemann, World Shapers (Wheaton: Harold Shaw Publishers, 1991), p. 74.
5. Paul S. Minear, *Eyes of Faith* (Westminister Press, 1946), p. 19.
6. Richard R. DeRidder and Roger S. Greenway, *Let the World Know* (Grand Rapids, MI: Baker Book House, 1988), p 162.

seven

Trouble Free

"Our world can be moved Godward only by leaders who
have shared to a deep degree the heartbreak as He looks in
compassion and love on the world. Until you sense the
suffering tears in the **heart of God**, until you share to
some extent our Savior's suffering passion in Gethsemane,
until you come close enough to God to enable the Spirit to
yearn within you with His infinite and unutterable yearning,
you are not prepared to minister about the cross."[1]
Wesley L. Duewel

Daniel, Shadrach, Meshach and Abednego were missionaries by force. They never
volunteered and said, "Sign me up. I want to go do mission work in Babylon."
They just got taken there, but God had His purposes. There are many stories of
how God used them to influence kings in order to bless the nations.

The stories surrounding these servants of the Most High are foundational to our
Sunday School curriculum. Most of us are familiar with God's salvation and
protection, while they were in captivity. Though the stories all had the immediate
fruit of saving an individual(s),
look again, and you still see clearly that these events had the ultimate goal of
making God's Name known to the nations.

Though He Slay Me
You remember: Shadrach, Meshach and Abednego would not bow down, and so
they were thrown into the furnace. Nebuchadnezzar asked them, "Is your God
really worth it? Can he save you?" They responded, "Well, He can save us, but
we don't know if he will. Whatever the outcome, we're not going to bow down."
(Dan. 3:15-18) Oh how we need Christians like that in today's Church! We could
turn the world upside down once again. "Though He slay me, yet will I follow."
(Job 13:15)

43

A Muslim mullah would have never believed in Jesus except through that "though He slay me" spirit exhibited through two grieving parents.

The Mullah was distraught when his misguided son stabbed three Christians to death on a railway station platform. Two of the dead were Pakistani nurses. The third was the only son of a missionary couple. The Mullah groaned inwardly, as he went to visit the bereaved missionary parents.

It was better than he thought, for when he listened to them, instead of condemning him, they sought to comfort him. They told him of a peace in their hearts, which Jesus Christ had given them. This peace surely passed understanding, but finally the Mullah understood. He found Jesus Christ for himself, and then — out of gratitude to his Savior — became a Christian pastor. Today he proclaims the Gospel that he once despised.[2]

This is the type of Christianity that is largely missing from our churches. We hear the mantras of contemporary, selfish theology that say "You are a child of the King, and you don't have to take any suffering or hardship. If only you demand your rights, you will be delivered." In our demanding, I wonder if we are saying, "Jesus I won't follow you unless it is nice and cozy, safe and warm, healthy and prosperous." It is a good thing that these three boys did not think that way. They looked square at Nebuchadnezzar and said, "It doesn't matter if He will save us, though we know He can. We would prefer to die than to bow to your compromise!"

Fire Insurance

Nebuchadnezzar said, "Pfhh! Throw them in, and make it hotter, 'cause I' m mad now!" The burly guards who threw them in were burned to a crisp right there at the door, and these three "religious rebels" started walking around in the fire. Then there were four of them — the Lord was among them. Nebuchadnezzar was impressed. . . astonished is more likely. He stuttered, "Come out. I want to talk with you." God had preserved Shadrach, Meshach and Abednego.

Was it for their own sake that they were preserved? Of course God loved them, but Shadrach and friends, though at the center of the drama, were not the reason for the drama. If it were only about them, God was well able to save them before all this. Instead, God let them go into the fire as a testimony to Nebuchadnezzar, and through him, to the ends of the earth:

Therefore I make a decree that any people, nation, or language which speaks anything against the God of Shadrach, Meshach and Abednego shall be cut in pieces, and their houses shall be made an ash heap; because there is no other God who can deliver like this (Dan. 3:29).

Do you see what is going on here? Israel, the local kicking dog, has been exalted to a place where people can not even say a word against their God. They can not even whisper it; not even think it. The miracle of Shadrach, Meshach and Abednego caused this sudden shift. This had to have caused a minor uproar in the kingdom. It would be like Hitler during WWII suddenly saying the Jews were now to be respected and that no one could say anything negative toward them and their God. Anyone caught profaning the God of Abraham would be thrown in the gas chamber.

As this message went throughout the kingdom, people must have said,

> "Who are Shadrach, Meshach, and Abednego?"
> "Well, let me tell you the story. You remember the idol. "Bow" was the command. They would not bow. They were thrown in the fire. The King saw four! He commanded them to come out. They didn't smell bad at all."
> "Are you serious? I mean, this is a joke, right?"
> "No. Don't say anything. This could cost you your life."

Suddenly, the God of Shadrach, Meshach and Abednego had exalted Himself above every other deity, because no other god can save like He can.

They Didn't Come Back

I was in a retirement home in San Diego, telling a group about my recent adventures in China with the underground church. Afterwards a man approached me and told me that he had been Nate Saint's supervisor and had signed off on his plans to reach a remote and fierce tribe in Ecuador. Nate and four other missionaries were working to reach this unevangelized tribal group deep in the jungle.

After several positive indications that this tribe would receive them, the men left their wives and children behind and headed back into the jungle to make personal contact with one village that they had discovered. All five never returned. As wives waited anxiously, others went to search for the missing men, only to find their speared and lifeless bodies on the shore of some nameless river, deep in the jungle.

As my new friend retold me the story, the gap of years vanished and the pain welled up fresh in his eyes. If only he had not agreed to the plan, perhaps they would still be alive, and all those children would have had their fathers. He confessed to the darkness that crowded his soul, until Jesus revealed His hand in the matter.

Trouble Free

The year was 1956 and the newspapers all cried out about the terrible waste of men in their prime. Nevertheless, as Tertullian said in around AD 200, "The blood of martyrs is seed for the Church."[3] Two things happened: A wave of young people stood to follow the trail of these five martyrs. Also the tribe ended up turning to Christ through the ongoing labor of two family members of the martyrs, Nate Saint's sister, Rachel, and Jim Elliot's wife, Elizabeth. Imagine taking your children to live among the very people who had murdered your husband. God was glorified even in their deaths. He exalted His Name and Character above all other gods through the willing sacrifice of His servants.

Two different groups of young men went into the fire, and only one came out. Was one group lacking in faith? No. We belong to Jesus, and we are His to do with as He pleases, so that He may be glorified by our life or even by our death. Our safety is not the big deal; it is our obedience that places us in the category of usefulness. Jim Elliot wisely said before his death, "He is no fool who gives what he cannot keep to gain what he cannot lose."[4] Through our life or death, Jesus has the platform He needs to proclaim the greatness of His Name and Character, as a testimony to the nations.

Our Lives, Their Bible

After church, a group of my good friends went over to Zorba's for a bite to eat. This was a great restaurant for all lovers of gyros and the like. Everyone who worked there was a nominal Muslim from Iran. I loved to frequent there just to develop relationships and to see if Jesus might not give me opportunity to speak of Him.

On this Sunday night after we had eaten, everyone began leaving, and our daughter, Jessica, who was three at the time, stood at the door, waving goodbye to all her friends. Somehow she slipped her little hand into the backside of the heavy glass door, as it slowly closed. With a terrifying scream of pain she summoned us to her rescue. After we reopened the door, the damage was evident. Her hand looked crushed. Deep indentations marked all across the dark purple wounds.

As Jessi cried out in agony, immediately our good friends rushed to pray for her. I remember my wife praying for peace, that God would bring His peace to Jessi and calm her down. Instantly Jessica stopped crying and just rested in her mother's arms. We then began to pray that Jesus would heal and restore what had been damaged. Before our eyes this poor crushed hand of my little girl was restored to perfect health.

We had been praying rather loudly; it was not the time for timidity. We had forgotten that there were others in the establishment, let alone Muslims. As I turned to get more ice for her hand, I noticed that every Muslim in that restaurant had gathered at the counter, or were sticking their heads through the kitchen window, straining to see what was happening. With wide, unbelieving eyes, they were transfixed by this unfolding drama. One young man named Nadiman reached across the counter and grabbed my shirt demanding, "Are you a Christian?" I said, "Yes," and he, with solemn honor in his voice, proclaimed before the whole group, "I want to become one!"

Where did that come from? For several years I had been befriending them, talking to them, even trying to introduce them to Jesus, all with seemingly no affect, until this incident with Jessi. Now God had their attention. He had distinguished Himself from mere talk to God! How? Through the lives of His servants. Are you willing to let Him place you on the platform of drama, impossible situations that demand dramatic rescues? Or do you prefer the illusion of your "in control" life that pretty much doesn't need God, and looks just like your secular, yet moral neighbor? W.J. Toms warns, "Be careful how you live; you may be the only Bible some person ever reads."[5]

Nebuchadnezzar Converts

Did you know that Nebuchadnezzar wrote scripture? We always talk about Nebuchadnezzar being the perfect type of the really bad guy, but all of Daniel Chapter 4 is scripture that he wrote. It is like a tract that he sent out to all the nations.

> Nebuchadnezzar, the King. To all peoples, nations, and languages that dwell in the earth . . . (Dan. 4:1).

He sent this beyond his kingdom's boundary. He wanted people everywhere to know this good news. What news? The tract talks about how he went crazy for seven years, and then how at the end of that time his senses returned to him, because he praised God and gave honor to Him. He had fallen because of His pride. He repented and exalted God, and God returned his sanity to him and, an even greater trouble free miracle, God returned His kingdom to him. This chapter is his testimony to the one great God, and it ends with:

> Now I, Nebuchadnezzar, praise and extol and honor the King of heaven, all of whose works are truth, and His ways justice. And those who walk in pride He is able to put down (Dan. 4:37).

He is testifying about our God. The peoples of the world did not have the Bible then. All they had were these little edicts that were sent out by Nebuchadnezzar and other kings, and this little tract was sent out to all the nations of the known world.[6] If anyone was curious about God, he was getting little scripture portions, and they could ask questions. He could grab a Jew and say, "Tell me more about your God." God was making His Name known.

Trouble Free

Daniel in the Lions' Den

It is hard to find a more beloved Old Testament story than Daniel and the Lions' Den. It is the best of drama! Here, God's chosen servant for years, through the reign of several kings and several kingdoms, faces his greatest challenge: the lions!

You remember that Daniel was thrown in the lions' den, because some jealous individuals tricked Darius, whose kingdom was larger than any other kingdom before. Darius made a rule that no gods other than him could be worshiped for thirty days. Daniel would not compromise, and in full view of the people he prayed to the one true God, as He always had done. Darius was required to follow his own edict, and sadly had to throw Daniel in the lions' den; but Daniel survived! Pioneer missionary, T.J. Bach, knew about the lion's den and wrote, "Safety does not depend on our conception of the absence of danger. Safety is found in God's presence, in the center of His perfect will."[7] Darius came out the next morning and said, "Daniel, has your God saved you?" Daniel replied, "Yeah, I'm still here," so the king pulled him up and made this decree:

> Then King Darius wrote: To all peoples, nations, and languages that dwell in all the earth; Peace be multiplied to you. I make a decree that in every dominion of my kingdom men must tremble and fear before the God of Daniel. For He is the living God, and steadfast forever; His kingdom is the one which shall not be destroyed. And His dominion shall endure to the end. He delivers and rescues, and He works signs and wonders in heaven and on earth, Who has delivered Daniel from the power of the lions (Daniel 6:25-27).

Everywhere this went, to all these languages, tongues, tribes and nations, do you know what the people were doing? They were begging for more information:

> "Tell me more. So Daniel was thrown in the lions' den and he survived overnight?'
> "Yeah, he survived."
> "Well maybe the lions weren't hungry."
> "No, they were hungry. The scoundrels who tricked the king were thrown in, and they were eaten up before they even hit the ground."

God was exalting Himself again through this supernatural testimony. Why? Because there is no other Name under heaven by which men might be saved.

Can I Get a Testimony?

You know that God could have saved Daniel before the lions' den. He is, after all, all-powerful! He could have done it, but He allowed Daniel to go through the lions' den, so that His Name would be made known. He also allowed Shadrach, Meshach and Abednego to go through the fire for the purpose of exalting His Name. He wants us to be the kind of believers in Him who will have an unfaltering and pure faith in the One, True Jehovah God — that in the face of all adversity, we will still look to and point to Him. Then, when God comes through, with no human explanation available, people will say, "Your God is different. Your God is real." And you can respond, "Yes, He's real. He's the only reason I am here today."

Paul and Silas were in prison singing at the top of their lungs — not the victorious life in some people's estimation. To many contemporary Christians, God's protection is supposed to keep you out of those kinds of places. How different New Testament Christianity is from its contemporary Western imitation. When faced with persecution and death, we now would cry out, "Save us from this temporary hardship," whereas Paul and Silas asked God for boldness to proclaim Christ. I have heard some foolishness, like: "They didn't know how to fight the supernatural battle," or "They didn't claim their rights as King's kids." Contrary to that, Paul and Silas were there by the plan of God. They were on the stage of drama. Sure, God could have snuck them out at midnight, but they were okay with death too, even as James was never rescued. (Acts 12:2) When God shook the place violently, everyone could have run free. The earthquake was not for their escape. They became the vessels that brought salvation to a desperate man and his family. This is a missionary tradition. Through our lives, God dramatically gives a testimony that plants the church among the unreached.

The key was that they were vessels willing to be broken and spilled out for their God — whether by life or death, they were His. This is the commitment we need to make. When offered the best the world had to offer, Daniel "***purposed in his heart***" (Daniel 1:8) that he would follow God alone. Daniel was a man after God's own heart. This is what made Daniel a man like few others — in power and influence on earth, and intimacy and secret sharing with God.

Notes:
1. Wesley L. Duewel, *Ablaze For God,* (Grand Rapids: Francis Asbury Press, 1989), p. 238.
2. David Brainerd Woodward, *God, Men and Missions,* (Gospel Light Publications, 1964), pp. 4-5.
3. Frank S. Mead, *Encyclopedia of Religious Quotations* (London: Peter Davies Ltd., 1965), p. 300.
4. Elizabeth Elliot, *Shadow of the Almighty,* (New York: Harper & Brothers, Publisher, 1958), p. 15.
5. Mead, *Encyclopedia of Religious Quotations,* (London: Peter Davies Ltd. 1965), p. 33.
6. Of all the Old Testament writers, Nebuchadnezzar's tracts/Scripture portions were perhaps the most widely read and translated into more languages than any other. The Gospel according to Nebuchadnezzar (Dan. 4) and other kingly testimonials (as what came from Darius regarding Daniel) were the only Scripture much of the ancient/non-Jewish world had before the translation of the Septuagint.
7. Vinita Hampton and Carol Plueddemann, *World Shapers*, (Wheaton: Harold Shaw Publishers, 1991), p. 73.

eight

Adam Version 1.75

> "We all want to do the will of God, and we know that
> there is nothing nearer to **His heart** than
> the evangelization of the world."[1]
> Oswald J. Smith

We in the Western church seem to have an allergic reaction when it comes to the commands of Jesus to go.

> Ko-Chat-Thing, a Karen convert from Burma, when in (America) was asked to preach to a congregation regarding their obligation to send out missionaries. After a moment of thought, he asked with a good deal of emotion: "Has not Christ told them to do it?"
>
> "Oh yes," was the reply, "But we wish you'd remind them of their duty."
>
> "Oh no!" said the Karen; "If they will not mind Jesus Christ, they will not mind me."[2]

No, we probably wouldn't. If we will not listen to Moses or the prophets, if we will not hear Him who rose from the grave, whom will we hear?

A follower of Jesus needs to become accustomed to the "Go" command. It has been a repeating theme of His all the way through scripture. From the very first humans to the present, He has been telling us to *"Go,"* and our disobedience has been a "complimentary" reality. A.W. Tozer saw this clearly,

> There is what William James called "a certain blindness in human beings" that prevents us from seeing what we do not want to see. This, along with the direct work of the devil

himself, may account for the fact that the doctrine of obedience is so largely neglected in modern religious circles. That God expects us to be "obedient children" is admitted, of course, but it is seldom stressed sufficiently to get action. Many people seem to feel that our obligation to obey has been discharged by the act of believing on Jesus Christ at the beginning of our Christian lives."[3]

I have seen a healthy and growing church turn away from obedience to the command to *"Go."* They started to pursue other things, and soon they were an empty and dying church. They had lost their way in denying the urgency to obey the command to *"Go."* S. D. Gordon knew this and said, "If we lose the spirit of 'go,' we have lost the very Christian spirit itself. *A disobedient church will become a dead church. It will die of heart failure."*[4] The late Oswald Smith was heard saying, "If the church is sick, put it on a missionary diet."[5] Perhaps the problem with our churches will not be solved by a new purpose to drive us, or figuring out what "unchurched Harry" wants us to do, but by obedience to our Master's command to *"Go!"*

Adam Number One

God created man, and the very first command that He gave to Adam and Eve is in Genesis 1:28:

> And God blessed them, and God said to them, "Be fruitful and multiply; fill the earth and subdue it; have dominion over the fish of the sea, over the birds of the air, and over every living thing that moves on the earth."

God created man to be lord of creation or vice-regent with limited autonomy. He was to have partnership in ruling on the earth, and God commanded them to "be fruitful, multiply and fill the earth." Along came a glitch, a little fruit problem — sin. Glitch is the most appropriate title, because God was not saying, *"Ooh, let's make man, and they'll sin. Then we can try and rescue them."* God did not intend or desire that man sin. However, knowing that man would, God prepared a rescue.[6] Sin is a glitch. It is something to be overcome. Just as the first Adam originally threw us all into this problem of sin, the second Adam, which is Jesus Christ, rescues us from the problem of sin and restores that right relationship with God. Through His blood, He rescues us from the glitch of sin, so that we can again have relationship with God, like Adam and Eve did in the garden before the fall. He makes it possible for us to walk in His original purposes for us of ruling and reigning with Him.

Adam Version 1.5

Sin entered the picture, and things got messy. This rebellious group continued to sin, until God was sorry He even made them, so He "nuked" them — with the flood. He wiped them all out and started over with Noah and His family. Like a Microsoft product, Noah became Adam 1.5. (Remember, Jesus was the glitch free Adam 2.0.) After their dramatic rescue and successful landing, God gave Adam 1.5 and his family a command:

> So God blessed Noah and his sons, and said to them: "Be fruitful
> and multiply, and fill the earth" (Gen. 9:1).

It is a repeat of Genesis 1:28. Just because sin entered the equation did not mean that God said, *"Oh, I've got to scrap all my plans for mankind."* He still had the same plan — be fruitful, multiply and fill the earth. It is very New Testament sounding to me. Be fruitful: "If you abide in me, you will bear much fruit." Multiply: "Go and make disciples." Fill the earth: "Of all nations." Jesus' purpose for the redeemed is still summated in "Be fruitful, multiply and fill the earth."

The Tower

Time moves on again to Genesis 11. You know this story. Man rebelled again. They built a tower. Do you remember what your Sunday School teacher told you was the reason they built the tower? They were trying to reach God, right? Everything I know about God says that is probably the correct interpretation. They were building, and God was saying, *"Oh my goodness! Look how big that is! That is tall! It's almost here! Think, God. What are you going to do when they get here? Come on, God, think, think, think — I know. I will bring confusion! Whew! That was close, one more brick and . . ."* No! Who is going to build a mountain tall enough to get to God?

I have heard another explanation for it. This is from the theological realms. They have thought it out. "Well, they understood that judgment was coming soon, and so, in order to escape the judgment they so rightly deserved, they decided to build a very tall mountain in the middle of their city, so they could all escape the impending flood. After all, that was how God did it the last time." Neither of these two explanations is in scripture. What does it say?

> And they said, "Come let us build ourselves a city, and a tower
> whose top is in the heavens; let us make a name for ourselves,
> **lest we be scattered abroad over the face of the whole earth**"
> (Gen. 11:4).

Let us build a tower that is really tall — for what purpose? First, it was "to make a name for ourselves." This is kind of odd. Verse one of this chapter says that there is only one people on the earth, and they are all gathered here on this plain. There was no one else for whom to show off, so this was plain old arrogance against God. Then the number two reason was "lest we be scattered abroad over the face of the whole earth" — rebellion against the first command and command number 1.5: "Be fruitful, multiply and fill the earth." They were rebelling against the purpose of God.

Here is where we can learn something. God was really intent on getting them to the ends of the earth. *When man rebels against the purposes of God, He forces compliance.* You may not like the sound of that. But it is true. We see the first example of it right here. We will examine this important principle later, but this needs to be understood for the rest of Scripture and history, past and present. God is the same God! When man says, "No, we won't go," God says, *"Yes, you will."*[b]

Arguing With Your General

God desires our obedience. He is our great Commander-in-Chief, and there really should be no discussion about whether or not to go. I think that we need to view this in light of the military. Before my father found Jesus, he served as a Drill Sergeant in the US Marines during the Korean War. This has always made discipline an interesting issue in our home. If there was one thing for sure, I did not dispute with the "officer in charge" (known as "Dad" in civilian families). I have read about the officer who had received orders from the Duke of Wellington. This officer unwisely complained that it was impossible to carry them out. Wellington replied, "I did not ask your opinion; I gave you my orders and expect them to be obeyed." Implicit obedience is required of every soldier of Jesus Christ. Robert Morrison, the first Protestant missionary to China, observed of the church almost 200 years ago:

> They say, "Souls are of equal value everywhere: there are plenty of pagans and of unconverted souls in this country; and while these are unconverted and unsaved, what is the use of going into other nations. Home is dear to us. English souls are as valuable as Hindu souls. If I can save five souls a year here, I shall be more useful here than some of the Missionaries, who have labored twenty years, without perhaps saving one soul, or but one or two."

> To this mode of speaking I am really at a loss what to say. It seems pious, but I fear it is impious sophistry, virtually impugning the wisdom and goodness of the Savior's command, to make known His salvation to all nations. I conceive the Savior's declared intentions and wishes must be the rule to individual disciples and churches. And while there are many nations to whom Christ's salvation has not been proclaimed; the reasoning which has been exhibited is impertinent and irrelevant. Oh! man, who art you that argues against your Savior? He says, "Go

and disciple all nations"— but you say, "No: we will stay till all the souls in this nation are converted." Here I might ask, on what system of theology is the opinion grounded, that such will ever be the case with respect to any one nation? Would that this were the case! But many men will not come to Christ, that they may be saved. Broad is the road that leads to destruction, and multitudes persist in travelling onward in it.

"What our Savior taught, and did, and suffered on earth, was for the benefit of all nations. And it is His revealed will that the glad tidings of salvation should be proclaimed to *all nations*. If this suffice not, Oh you ministers and Christians, to sanction, and to stimulate, and to encourage your going, I have done; my arguments are exhausted. If required obedience to the Almighty Savior will not operate on ministers and churches, I know not *"by what methods,"* nor *"by what topics to excite them to Missionary exertions."*[6]

Eternal Babel?

Sometimes we look at the tongues, tribes and nations that came out of the Tower of Babel as part of God's judgment. We look at the missionary task and groan at the complexity of learning languages and overcoming the daunting barriers of culture that initiated at the tower. However, the world's cultures are not a judgment of God; they are a creation of God. They were always His design. They were something He desired to see happen among people. He wanted the people to spread out over planet earth. I think there were a couple of reasons. One is that He created the whole world, and it was great! He really wanted mankind, His partner, His eternal Bride, to enjoy it with Him. The other reason is that if one takes any language group and divides them geographically, separating them for a time, unique cultures and even different languages will develop.

God loves the cultures of the world. You know how I know this? Look what we see in heaven — "every tongue, tribe and nation standing before the throne." It is not as if we get to heaven and God says, *"Check your culture in here. That goes to hell."* No. He preserves it for all eternity, and we can still see the language groups, the tribes, the nations. God loves culture. John Piper in His book, *Let the Nations Be Glad*, gives a convincing argument using a choir as the example. It sounds nice when the choir all sings in unison, but how much more beautiful it sounds when they suddenly split into harmony. So also, the worship of many cultures before the throne is like a harmony.[7] People groups each worship God in a unique way, a beautiful way that no other does. I think I will want to hang out with each tongue, tribe and nation for a couple of million years, celebrating Jesus. Culture is not a bad thing; it is a God thing!

Military Tactics

When God brought the flood, it was the "nuke 'em" strategy. At the Tower of Babel, we begin to see tactical military strategy. The Chinese book *The Sun Tze*, which is the oldest military treatise known, says: "When faced with a large, unified opponent, divide and conquer."[8] (Not "run like mad." That is a different book.) Divide and conquer. We have been using it ever since. During the Gulf War, we used this strategy. In Iwojima, the marines used it. It is the maxim of warfare — divide the enemy into small units, and then as a larger unit, you have superiority. God did this. He took this unified group of humankind that was rebellious against Him, His purposes and His desires, and He divided them. Was it for the purpose of obliteration? No. It was for the purpose of reconquering them, taking them back one by one, people group by people group.

Adam Version 1.75?

In order to start recapturing the scattered, newly formed language groups of the world; God called Abram in Genesis Chapter 12 to mobility. The first word out of God's mouth to Abram is, *"Go!"* Get accustomed to God saying, *"Go."* **Check this out: He says it over 1,600 times in the Bible**. The Bible only says "stay" a couple hundred times, and most of the places you find "stay," it is said by those who are trying to get God's people not to obey.[c] It is this way in Scripture, because God knows our nature. He knows that when it comes down to it, we are homebodies. We kind of like sticking together in Babel. We like to stay with our own kind, our father's household, our people, our food, so God says, *"Go!"*

The choice of Abraham was not God giving up on humanity and dealing with Israel only. This is not Adam 1.75 — *"Forget everyone else; I will start over with you!"* Rather, it was a beachhead. It was the beginning of a military campaign to retake the peoples of the world one at a time. From this one man, God promised to bless every family of people.

We, who are God's people, are to be mobile, to fill the whole earth. It is *all* His domain. In Psalms 2:8-9, David is hearing an interaction between God, the Father, and Jesus. God says, "Ask of me, and I will give the nations for Your inheritance, and the ends of the earth for Your possession. You shall rule them with a rod of iron." This is part of that "going to the ends of the earth and ruling and reigning with Christ" that we saw back in Genesis 1. But you say, "That was said to Jesus." In Revelation, Jesus turns around and says the same thing to us — that if we ask, He will give the nations as our possession and we will rule them. (Rev. 2:26-27) We, God's people, are to claim the whole earth and nothing less than that.

There is a term in "Christianese" called *sojourner*. It came from the idea that this earth is not my home; I am just passing through. Heaven is my home. I have no roots here. Wherever the Master wants me to go, I will go. Possessions do not mean anything to me. Whatever He wants to do with them is fine. This is not my home. We do not use the term *sojourner* much anymore. It has lost its meaning. Let me give you a better one — how about *bedouin*, someone who travels around — a *nomad*. It is somebody who takes his or her things, rolls them up on the back of a camel and goes where the grazing is good for the sheep. It is someone who is mobile. This is to be the nature of God's people. He is our Leader. He is the one who establishes where we should go.

A Personal Call

If you wait for the lightning bolt from heaven, assuring you that the general call to all Christians everywhere in all times to "Go and make disciples of all nations" was meant specifically for you, you may sadly never get it. We are all called to "Go", the specifics of where and how are the only issues. Scripture says plainly to "Go," not to stay. If you are "staying" without a specific word from the Lord to stay, you may be in disobedience. Are you presuming, "He knows my number; if He wants me to minister in deep, dark Cambodia, He can call"? Perhaps He already has, and you assumed it was not for you.

The heresy that we each need a lightning bolt is part of the reason that half the world remains in total darkness two thousand years after the command to "Go" was given. Robert Savage, missionary to Ecuador, states boldly:

> The command has been to "go," but we have stayed — in body, gifts, prayers and influence. He has asked us to be witnesses unto the uttermost part of the earth . . . but 99% of Christians have kept puttering around in the homeland.[9]

A fresh Marine recruit was on the drill field for the first time. The drill sergeant bellowed out, "Ten-shun!" Immediately, all of his squad snapped to attention, waiting for the next order. Then came the next command, "Forward, march!" Everybody stepped forward — everybody, except the fresh recruit. The sergeant rubbed his eyes in disbelief. He brought everyone to a halt and stomped over to the marine, which was still, amazingly, standing at attention. Grabbing the recruit's right ear, the sergeant put his mouth close to it and bellowed,
"Does this thing work?"
"Yes, sir," the marine replied.
The sergeant marched to the other side, pulled that ear and yelled,
"How about this ear? Does it work?"
Again the marine said, "Yes, sir!"
"Did you hear me when I said, 'Forward, march'?"
"Yes, sir!"
"Then kindly tell me why in the world didn't you move out with the rest of the squad?"
The young recruit responded in amazement, "Oh, did you mean me, sir? I didn't hear my name."[10]

Adam Version 1.75

I know a lot of people who are waiting for the lightening bolt that comes out of the sky accompanied by a loud, "Go." Why is it that they need no lightening bolt to stay in their current job? We all need to seek God to find out what He wants us to do. He is the one who sends us where He wants us to be, but we have to submit to Him and ask, "Where do you want me?" The raw fact is that most people never even open themselves up to hearing the missionary "Go." Through fear or the rejection of previous insight, they all but guarantee that they will never be "called."

Robert Hall Glover says it rightly:

> The call to military service furnishes illustration of what we are seeking to emphasize respecting missionary service. This country when at war declares a draft of man power, in terms of which every man of military age and fitness is conscripted for active service. The norm is to go, not to stay. The only honorable exempts from going are those disqualified for overseas service, or those who can serve their country's cause better by remaining at home. Exactly so should it be in the Church's missionary war. In view of Christ's imperative "GO" and the overwhelmingly greater need in the foreign fields than at home, loyalty to Him and love for lost souls constitute a compelling claim upon all Christians whose age, health, qualifications, and providential circumstances admit of it, to answer the call in person and "endeavor to GO," while all others should "GO" by prayer and purse, to the full measure of their ability.[11]

Abraham is the Father of our Faith — you know the song, "Father Abraham had many sons, many sons had Father Abraham. I am one of them, and so are you . . . ." If you are one of the children of Abraham, then he is the Father of our Faith. The same mobility to which he was called is essential for us to have.

Notes
a. Theology is sometimes a walk on slippery rocks, and someone is always eager to give you a "helpful" push. I am not addressing issues of foreknowledge and preparation (1Pet. 1:20, Rev. 13:7), though I am mindful of these discussions. I am simply addressing the original desires of God regarding His plans for mankind.
b. I know that this a potentially dangerous chapter. First I made the Reformists mad, and now the Wesleyans will be uptight. If you feel left out, I am sure there is something for you in future chapters.
c. (Thanks to my fellow missionary zealot, Dwayne Weehunt.)
1. Oswald J. Smith, *The Passion for Souls,* (London: Marshall, Morgan and Scott, Ltd., 1950), p. 79.
2. Augustus C. Thompson, *Foreign Missions,* (New York: Charles Scriber's Sons, 1889), p. 62.
3. A. W. Tozer, *This World: Playground or Battleground?,* (Camp Hill, PA: Christian Publication, 1989), p.71.

4. S. D. Gordon, *What Will It Take to Change the World,* (Grand Rapids: Baker Book House, 1979), p. 66.

5. Oswald J. Smith, *The Challenge of Missions,* (London: Star Books, 1959), p. 126.

6. Robert Morrison, *A Parting Memorial,* (London: W. Simpkin and R. Marshall, 1826), p. 309-310.

7. John Piper, *Let the Nations Be Glad,* (Grand Rapids, MI: Baker Books, 1993), p. 216.

8. *The Sun Tze* (Taipei, Taiwan: Confucius Publishing Co. B.C. 510).

9. Vinita Hampton and Carol Plueddemann, *World Shapers,* (Wheaton: Harold Shaw Publishers, 1991), p. 5.

10. James M. Weber and Don Wardell, *Let's Quit Kidding Ourselves About Missions,* (Winona Lake, IN: 1979), p. 57.

11. Robert Hall Glover, *The Bible Basis of Missions,* (Los Angeles: Bible House of Los Angeles, 1946), pp. 139-140.

nine

Who Will Go?

"How He must be longing for anybody whom He can pick
up to satisfy His great **heart** of love, in gathering in
multitudes of the lost."[1]
D. E. Hoste

Dr Duff was a great pioneer missionary in India. He spent 25
years there preaching the Gospel and establishing schools. He
came back with a broken down constitution. He was permitted
to address the General Assembly at Edinburgh in 1867 in order
to make an appeal for men to go to the mission field. After he
had spoken for a considerable time, he became exhausted and
fainted away . . . They carried him out of the Hall into another
room . . . The doctors carefully attended him for some time, and
at last he began to recover.

When he realized where he was, he roused himself and said, "I
did not finish my speech; carry me back and let me finish it."
They told him he could only do it at the peril of his life. Said he
. . . "I will do it or die."

They took him back to the Hall. It was one of the most solemn
scenes ever witnessed: They brought the white-haired man into
the Assembly Hall, and as he appeared at the door, every person
sprang to his feet; the tears flowing freely as they looked upon
the grand old Veteran.

With a trembling voice he said, "Fathers and Mothers of
Scotland, is it true that you have no more sons to send to India
to work for the Lord Jesus Christ? The call for help is growing
louder and louder, but there are few coming forward to answer

it. You have the money put away in the bank, but where are the laborers who shall go into the fields?

. . . Turning to the President of the assembly he said, "Mr. Moderator, if it is true that Scotland has no more sons to give to the service of the Lord Jesus Christ in India, although I have lost my health in that land and come home to die, if there are none who will go and tell those heathen of Christ, then I will be off tomorrow, to let them know that there is one old Scotchman who is ready to die for them. I will go back to the shores of the Ganges and there lay down my life as a witness for the Son of God."[2]

The millions of unreached peoples of the mountains of North India, the jungles of South East Asia and China, the Muslims of Central Asia and North Africa call out for help, and with our God we in one voice ask, "Who will Go?"

Some People Just Don't Want To
Where are the obedient ones who say "Here am I, send me. Though none go with me, yet I will follow." It is our responsibility to find a way or make a way to reach the unreached and obey the *"Go"* of Christ! However, throughout history, much of the Church has tried to wiggle out from under the mandate force of the Great Commission. Consider the German hymn that was very popular in the 1750's:

Of old 'twas said indeed,
'Go forth to every land,'
But tarry where thou art
is now the Lord's command.[3]

When Baptist ministers met in England in 1788, they heard a young preacher named William Carey stand and propose the "duty of Christians to attempt the spread of the Gospel among the heathen nations." The Chairman was so against this "missionary craziness'" that he jumped to his feet with a frown and thundered out, "Young man sit down! When God pleases to convert the heathen, He will do it without your aid or mine."[4]

No matter how some have tried to modify, or even repeal this command of Christ to "Go and make disciples of all nations," it stands. After all attempts to talk Leonard Dober, the first Moravian Missionary, out of his plans to take the Good News of Jesus to the unreached slaves of West India, he replied, "Even if no one should be benefited, and no fruits follow my efforts, yet I will go, for I must obey my Savior's call."[5]

It seems that many in the Church have turned a blind eye to the command of the

Savior. Robert Morrison felt this same frustration:

> Not only have Protestant efforts been vastly deficient; but even
> a mental recognition of the duty has been rare. Some years ago I
> looked over half a dozen Commentators on the (command to go);
> and found that they either passed over the great commandment
> to evangelize the nations, without notice, or slurred it over with
> a sentence or two, whilst pages were spent in arguing the time
> and manner of water baptism.[6]

Remember the principle: *When man rebels against God's orders, He forces compliance.* Like Jonah, the disciples rebelled. They spent all that time with Jesus, and yet they did not seem to understand. They heard it over and over again, "Be my disciples in Jerusalem, Judea, Samaria and the ends of the earth (Acts 1:8)," and yet eight chapters later they were still sitting around in Jerusalem. God allowed a great persecution to come upon the Church and forced them to spread out to the ends of the earth. (Acts 8:1)

This is not unusual. If we look at China in this light, we can understand a lot of what is happening. When the Communists took over China, most of the Christians, the Christian Universities and the areas that were largely evangelized were in the large cities. Then the Cultural Revolution came in the late 1960's, early 1970's, and the government tried to wipe out every vestige of foreign religion and foreign social order. They forced all of the city people to become country people, and they brought all the country people into the cities. They forced doctors and lawyers down and exalted janitors. It was a terrible time. City people do not know how to farm. There was mass starvation.

Before this time there were 2,000 ethnic groups in China (tongues, tribes and nations) that did not know anything about Jesus and had no churches among them. After the Cultural Revolution, there were only 900 ethnic groups left that had no Gospel witness.[7] Over half the job was done in roughly ten years, by God forcing the Christians out. They did not willingly go, but like Daniel, He forced them, and they were a powerful witness.

The Advance
We can understand history by this same principle. God did not stop working this way just because the Canon was complete. If the passion and concern of God has always been for the blessing to reach every tongue, tribe, and nation, then this gives us a significantly new paradigm by which to view history. Let us do a quick survey of history. The Romans controlled much of the world when Jesus was crucified. The Church kept growing, and the Romans could not stop it. They tried to stomp it out in one place, and it would spring up in another. It was in Spain; it was in Israel; it was in Persia; it was in Egypt. It was all over the place. It was not

just limited to one class of people. Slaves and their owners were turning to Jesus. It was in Rome. There were members of Caesar's own household that believed in that first generation. Though Constantine proclaimed Christianity the official religion of the Roman Empire, most historians say that within fifty years it would have been fact, even without his declaration. Christianity conquered the Roman Empire in those first four hundred years.

The Christians of Rome got complacent. They started arguing about theology, and they had all sorts of meetings to make sure that their theology was well defined. Then they threw the "heretics" out of the empire. The Romans actually built a wall in the north to keep the Germanic Barbarian tribes from coming down. Their missionary zeal was minimal to zero. They did not evangelize the northern tribes — the Germans, my ancestors, the pink people (red and yellow black and white and even us pink people are precious in His sight). Roman Christians did not recognize their obligation to evangelize the Barbarians to the North.

Gothic barbarians, Visigoths, Vandals, Germanic tribes (my people) crashed in upon the Christian world and settled among Christian people. Although the world viewed this from the human perspective that the great Roman Empire had fallen, God's concern was never for the Empire but for the peoples beyond who had never heard. He sacrificed the Roman Empire for the sake of His Kingdom expansion. The good news is that God so loved the German people, my people, that He allowed the Roman Empire to fall.

There was peace for a time. Then there came a dark age: the Vikings. The Norsemen were some violent people. It was not a centralized government with a unified attack that declared war on their southern neighbors. Rather, little tribes, even little villages would set off with a war party and go raid England. They slashed and burned and killed, and they especially picked on the churches. They also thought the southern women were gorgeous, so they carried back to their home priests and young ladies as servants and concubines. This was their mistake. Within a generation of each such raid, the mighty Vikings also succumbed to the power of Christianity.

Did God not love his daughters? Did God not watch out for them? He loved them, but as the Father sent Jesus, so sends He us. If He did not spare His own Son, do you think you are somehow above sacrifice? God's desire is for the Norsemen and the unreached of our world. Though it may not be the most pleasant situation into which He thrusts you, it is for His glory among the nations, that they might have life.[8]

The devastating Muslim invasion wiped out most of the healthy part of Christendom in North Africa, Persia and Turkey. The battles of the Crusades began. Somehow we got it in our minds that conquering by force was the best way to evangelize or "Christianize" the heathen. This strategy of power has never worked. It is the meek that shall inherit the earth.

There were some shining lights during this time, however. Francis of Assisi marched through both military lines straight up to the Caliph of Egypt with everybody watching in amazement. Francis proclaimed the Gospel to the Caliph who under conviction of the Holy Spirit said, "If I knew one other Christian like you, I would become one." All the Christians he knew were trying to kill him. Amazing.

The Crusades led way to the ends of the earth. Great discoveries were being made all around the world. Africa, Asia and India were explored. Christopher Columbus discovered the New World. Columbus felt that the Holy Spirit had impressed upon him that the voyage was possible, and he believed he was going for the sake of the Gospel. His original motive was to evangelize the people of the New World.[9]

As these discoveries were happening, God was touching the hearts of people in Europe, calling them to go as missionaries. The Moravians (1730's) were the first wave of Protestant missionaries. William Carey and Robert Moffat followed soon after. First they hit the coastlands, and they struggled to survive there. The missionaries of this era did not pack their belongings in crates or barrels. They packed them in their own coffins. When these missionaries waved goodbye to their loved ones, it was for the last time, and they knew it.

The average life expectancy of missionaries in this time was two years, and they poured into Africa. They were willing to lay down their lives to advance the Gospel inch by inch. One African king saw the missionaries unloading their coffins, and he said, "What is it that would drive them to sacrifice their lives on this foreign soil." He had to find out, and he became a Christian because of their testimony — "because they loved not their own life." The Gospel gained a foothold in Africa and stayed, and it advances on the blood of the martyrs even today.

Then came the inland missionaries like David Livingston, people who saw the vast interior. They saw the "smoke of a thousand villages" who had never heard the Name of Christ even once, and they could not go down to their graves letting it remain so. James Hudson Taylor pierced the darkness of inner China against incredible odds. He and those who followed after him expanded the Kingdom into regions that it had never been before.

In much of the history we have studied, God is just not there. Just as the sin of television is not the obvious evil, the cussing, the sex, the murder, it is the fact that it just almost entirely leaves out God. He is not mentioned. He is not given credit. He is not there. The same is true of our history books. However, the reality is that God *has* been there. He has been actively involved in history. These are not just some coincidental events packaged together. History is His story. It is God's story being revealed, and what is the story line about? What is the plot? It is God loving and bringing the world into right relationship with Him.

It is not too much to say that every major activity of God since the beginning of time has been a missionary venture. It had the ultimate purpose of making His Name known among the nations. Missions is the expressed will of God. It is the demonstrated activity of God in scripture and history. Missionary love is the revealed nature of God, and the salvation of lost peoples brings glory to God.

Yep, It is Still There

It is amazing how many of God's servants hear God say, *"Go."* Moses heard God say, "Go to Pharaoh, and tell Him to let My people go." Philip heard God say, "Go to the desert and minister to the Ethiopian." Jim West, Executive Director of Heart of God Ministries, and my father-in-law, has suggested tongue in cheek, *"Go* is so much of God's character that two-thirds of His name is *Go."*

God called Abraham to leave his people and go be a blessing to all nations. Jonah was called to go and warn the Ninevites. Jonah ran the other direction. He did not respond well when he heard the call to go. Ministering in Ninevah was his wildest fear, so he ran away. Most in our churches today never even hear the *"Go."* In fact, they fear it. Most Christians I talk to are afraid that God may call them to go as a missionary. Before God can even say the word *"Go,"* they've already run away from the job.

The Roman Centurion (Matt. 8:9) talked of people who are under authority, that go when they are told to go. I wonder, if we do not go, are we truly people under authority? God is not interested in our excuses. He is well aware of our shortcomings. Remember that is what Moses tried to do — wiggle out of God's call because of his shortcomings. God knows our shortcomings, and still He calls us to go. Charles Finney, the great evangelist, said,

> The plea of inability is the worst excuse. It slanders God so, charging Him with infinite tyranny in commanding men to do that which they have no power to do. All pleas and excuses for not submitting to God are acts of rebellion. It is not because they cannot do what God commands, but because they are unwilling.

Even as the Tower of Babel was, in essence, security for the people, and in some ways fame, a name for themselves, a long lasting reputation for generations to come, it was a direct opposite to the call of Abraham. He was called to leave security, but through it he would become the Father of Faith. That is the issue of faith, leaving security. Abraham left it. The people of Babel wanted security.

Jesus is calling His people, even as He did Peter, to get out of the boat and start walking on the water. Jesus is calling His people to cross the Jordan River and take the land.

Our lack of obedience to Him and His Great Commission, our lack of obedience to go where He calls us to go, might mean that we end up dying on the wrong side of the Jordan River.

I can see many Christians coming up to the seat of Christ on Judgment Day. He will say, *"You didn't obey the Great Commission,"* and they will argue, "But we did all these great things. We bought this organ for the church. We did this. We did that." And Jesus will respond, *"I desire obedience, not sacrifice. If you love me, you will obey my commands."* But they proved they did not love Him, because they did not obey His commands.

> *He who wins souls is wise.*
> *My son, if your heart is wise, My heart will rejoice!*
> *(Prov. 11:30, 23:15)*

Notes:

1. D. E. Hoste, "China's Millions," (London: Morgan & Scott, 1887), p. 125.
2. William Heslop, *Missionary Tidings,* (Greensboro: The Golden Rule Press, 1880's or 1890's), p. 41.
3. Frank S. Mead, *Encyclopedia of Religious Quotations,* (London: Peter Davies, Ltd. 1965), p. 54.
4. Ibid., p. 56.
5. Ibid., p. 59.
6. Morrison, *A Parting Memorial,* p. 308.

7. Though not a direct quote, the seed thought *(actually the whole tree!)* was planted in my mind by Roberta Winter who spoke in the class Perspectives On the World Christian Movement and by Ralph D. Winter, *Perspectives On the World Christian Movement,* "The Kingdom Strikes Back," (Pasadena: William Carey Library Publishers, 1992), p. B-3.
8. Winter, Roberta, Perspectives On the World Christian Movement class held in Bethany, Oklahoma, 1994.
9. Mission Frontier Bulletin, (Pasadena: U.S. Center for World Missions, Sept.- Dec. 1992), pp. 12-15.

ten

David and the Giant

"I firmly believe our greatest problem is not a lack of faith
or a lack of more teaching or a lack of better organization,
but our failure to fulfill the desire of the **heart of God** in
obeying the Great Commission."[1]
Kingsley Fletcher

"May the Lord impart to you **His heart**
for the unreached."[2]
C. Peter Wagner

One of our favorite stories is David and Goliath. It is found in 1 Samuel 17. The interpretation of David and Goliath in our time has often been "Are you in debt? Are you faced with the giant of bills? When you face those Goliath's, you can trust God to help you through it. God will defeat the giants with whatever is in your hand." Though that may be a valid spin on the event, it is not the interpretation that David understood and that the Holy Spirit preserved for us in scripture. David proclaimed exactly what God intended:

> This day the Lord will deliver you into my hand, and I will
> strike you and take your head from you. And this day I will give
> the carcasses of the camp of the Philistines to the birds of the air
> and the wild beasts of the earth, **that all the earth may know
> that there is a God in Israel** (1 Samuel 17:46).

My version, of course, reads a little bit differently: "Today, God will give you into my hands and we will smite you and your bodies will be given to the birds of the air and the beasts of the fields, so that all the world will know that God loves Israel and hates you dirty Philistines!" That is how I learned it in Sunday School. The impression I had was: Philistines are bad; Israelites are good. God hates Philistines. God loves Israelites.

David and the Giant

Is that what you see in the passage above? No! God loves the peoples of the world and jealously desires for them to be freed from their enslavement to demonic idols. This mighty miracle of God had less to do with saving Israel than it had to do with bringing God a reputation among the Philistines and in all the earth! If God only wanted to save Israel, He could have just made the giant get sick and die of worms (Acts 12:23) or something like that. No, God wanted to stack the odds impossibly against Israel that He might prove to the nations that He is the God of the Supernatural. There are none like Him. When Goliath hit the ground, the Philistines ran, and as far as they ran, this story went with them. As far as this tale was told, the God of the young boy was praised, and if anyone was curious, they discovered that the True God was the God of the Israelites.

"Shields on Maximum Power"
We know that if God had wanted to create some kind of force field around Israel that no army could penetrate, He could have. Long before this giant embarrassment happened, God could have just raised the shields that would have fried anyone who crossed the line, or at least given them a really good shock. But no, God put them in a place where they were constantly going to be invaded for this purpose: that the entire world would know. When God saved them miraculously, beyond human explanation, the nations would know that He alone is God. (Ex. 34:10) If God were just concerned about Israel being in right relationship with Him, pure, holy and undefiled, He would have put them in Siberia. Nobody invades Siberia. That is not what He had in mind for Israel:

> Thus says the Lord God: "This is Jerusalem; I have set her in
> the midst of the nations and the countries all around her" (Ez.
> 5:5).

Their invasion-prone placement was on purpose. God put Israel right in the middle of things. Any time Egypt wanted to invade Assyria or vice versa, they had to go through the local turnstile: Israel. Israel was constantly invaded, constantly bugged, constantly pestered, constantly traveled through, constantly impinged upon by foreigners and foreign belief systems, because God was more interested in the nations getting the blessing (Israel's very purpose for existence), than He was in just seeing that they were safe. God put them in the way of harm for His Name's sake.

Here again, little boy — giant Goliath, and everywhere that story spread, if anyone was hungry, if any Philistine noticed, "Hey, we keep losing these fights," they could turn to the one true God. They could see that the God of Israel was stronger than Baal. God was interested in exalting His Name above Baal's.

Wise Guy
David's son, Solomon, understood what was on God's heart. God blessed him

with wisdom and riches, and all the kings of the world sought audience with him (2 Chron. 9:22-23). Some speculate that Proverbs, Ecclesiastes, and Song of Solomon were handouts in his wisdom seminars. Solomon had the honor of building the temple his father had so wanted to build, and then he dedicated it. When something is dedicated, it means we set it apart or designate it for a specific purpose. In Solomon's dedication prayer for the temple, he states one of the central purposes of the temple:

> Moreover, concerning a foreigner, who is not of Your people Israel, but has come from a far country for Your name's sake (for they will hear of Your great name and Your strong hand and Your outstretched arm), when he comes and prays toward this temple, hear in heaven Your dwelling place, and do according to all which the foreigner calls to You, **that all the peoples of the earth may know** Your name and fear You, as do Your people Israel, and that they may know that this temple which I have built is called by Your name (1 Kings 8:41-43).

The temple was not just for Israel, but it was for the nations. Solomon had a great confidence that God was going to make His Name known among the nations. He said, "*When* they hear, because they will hear, and they will know that you are indeed God, hear their prayers, God."

Robert Morrison, while preparing to go as the first Protestant missionary to China, encountered one individual that was not at all encouraging.

> The man . . . looked at him with a smile that only half concealed his contempt, inquired, "Now, Mr. Morrison, do you really expect that you will make an impression on the idolatry of the Chinese Empire?" "No," said Morrison, "But I expect that God will."[3]

There is a confidence that comes in knowing that God desires to be known. That is why the Psalmist wrote to missionary zealots, "Be still and know that I am God, I will be known among the nations; I will be exalted among the heathen" (Ps. 46:10). Solomon knew of God's determination to make Himself known, so with confidence he could say, "When they hear of your great Name..."

House of Prayer for All Nations

Solomon believed so strongly that the temple was to be for the nations that almost half of the physical design of the temple was given to a court called "The Court of the Gentiles." Gentiles in Greek is the word *ethne*. In English this Greek root, *ethne*, formed the base of our word *ethnic*. Every time you read Gentile in your Bible, it means ethnics. Half of the temple was dedicated to The Court of the

Ethnics or The Court of the Nations. It was here that they could come and seek Him, pray to Him and submit themselves to the one true God.

The Law

Even in their law, the Israelites were to attract the nations. Its very purpose and the center of its design is God's desire to impress the nations with His righteousness and justice. God gave Israel a law that was unique in all the earth at the time. It was not like the Law Code of Hammurabi for the Mesopotamians that was cruel and harsh, rather it showed unusual mercy and kindness, especially to foreigners.

Hammurabi's Code was one of assuming people were guilty until proven innocent. In other words, an enemy could accuse you of a crime, and you would be guilty in a court of law unless you could prove yourself innocent. There were two ways you could prove your innocence: one was to provide witnesses or documentation in your favor, and the second was to submit to the test of the river. You would be placed in a chair and lowered into the Euphrates River. If you survived after being dunked several times, you validated your innocence. However, if you drowned, it only proved your guilt.

Orphans and widows were given almost no rights, aliens even worse. Yet Hammurabi's Code was acclaimed as the Great Law of the Middle East. The Law of God was different in character, nature, in justice and mercy. Those who were accused could find refuge for the sake of a fair hearing. In God's great law, we have justice given to the orphan and the widow. Full rights were extended to the alien living among the Israelites:

> Cursed is the one who distorts the justice due an alien, orphan
> or widow. And all the people shall say, "Amen" (Deut. 27:19).

Isaiah tells us that the purpose of the law was to show that God was righteous. God gave the law to help accomplish Gen. 12:1-3, to extend His blessing to every tongue, tribe and nation.

> Therefore be careful to observe them (the laws); for this is your
> wisdom and your understanding in the sight of the peoples
> (nations) who will hear all these statutes, and say, "Surely this
> is a wise and understanding people." For what great nation is
> there that has God so near to it, as the Lord our God is to us, for
> whatever reason we may call upon Him? And what great nation
> is there that has such statutes and righteous judgments as are in
> all this law which I set before you this day? (Deut. 4: 6-8)

The Festivals

Few would consider the law a place to find God's concern for all peoples, and even fewer would consider looking at the festivals of Israel as a revelation of God's love for all mankind. Nevertheless, even here, God puts little reminders all throughout Israel's religious life as to their obligation and duty and His love for the nations.

There were three festivals that all the males in Israel were required to attend (Ex.23:14-17). One was the Passover. The Passover was instituted back in Egypt when the Israelites put the blood of a lamb on the doorposts of their home. When the Angel of Death came to any house that had the blood on the doorposts, it passed by that home. We know that Jesus was crucified on the Passover, and we understand He was indeed the Lamb that was sacrificed for our salvation. He saved us from the Angel of Death and brought us out of slavery into freedom. He redeems us from sin and death. Even as every male had to participate in Israel, so it is now required for every person to acknowledge Jesus as the Passover Lamb.

The second feast was the Feast of Pentecost or the Feast of a Harvest Begun. It was a "First Fruit" celebration. The Israelites would go out as the harvest began and collect the first fruit off the trees and some of the first grain. They would bring them to the temple and wave them before the Lord in thanksgiving and supplication, asking God for a completed harvest. It was as though they were shouting, "More Lord! We're not satisfied! Give us more!" On the Day of Pentecost, we know what happened. The Holy Spirit was poured out upon the disciples in the upper room, and they received power and immediately went out and testified to men from all nations who were gathered in Jerusalem for this Feast of Pentecost. (Acts 2) In essence, God was saying, *"Here is first fruits of what I desire to have happen."* Let me quote my Vineyard brothers here. When we in agreement see the harvest that He has begun on planet earth, we say, "More Lord!"

Here were the first fruits of the global harvest, and it happened on the Day of Pentecost. What kind of fruit? Those who were redeemed by the blood *and* filled with His Spirit. (This issue alone deserves a book in and of itself; indeed many have been written.) Many people think they can get by with only attending the Feast of the Passover and skip Pentecost, as though it is optional. No! A hundred times, No! We are required to attend both! I have seen two problems in the Church today, both stinking of pride. The first is that we act like we do not need the Holy Spirit, His empowerment, transforming work, sanctifying grace, and imparted gifts. Some have almost retreated from the empowerment of the Holy Spirit to the extent that they are barely different from the Sadducees, who knew not the power of God, who continually wanted to make the Gospel of talk and not of dramatic power.

The second problem is this "once was enough for me" syndrome. How many of us have encountered saints who a long time ago (in a church far, far away) were filled with the Spirit, but have not felt Him move in that way since. They were desperate for more of God then, but have long since become "at ease" in Zion. This should not be! If the Apostles needed repeated fillings and empowerments, how much more do we? (Acts 4:31) It is not another seminar or methodology that we need to help us bring our churches back from the brink of death; it is a new Pentecost! These festivals were designed to be yearly reminders and yearly activities. We need fresh infillings of the Holy Spirit! Holy Spirit baptism is required. This is not up for discussion. (Acts 19:1-7) Not only are we required to put ourselves under the blood of Christ, but also we are required to have the baptism of the Spirit of Christ.

There was a third feast that all Israelite men were required to attend: the Feast of the Tabernacles, Booths or Tents. It is also called the Feast of the Ingathering. It was a feast of thanksgiving for the harvest completed. It was the most jubilant of all the festivals in Israel, a time of great joy and singing. On the first day, they gathered in the temple and faced the altar. With palm branches in their hands, they would stand in the Court of the Gentiles, singing and praising the Lord of the Harvest for the completed harvest.

Do you see the direct correlation between this festival and Revelation 7:9, where the people are standing before the throne of Jesus with palm branches in their hands, singing? This multitude is singing, "Worthy is the Lamb Who was slain and has redeemed us to God by Your blood out of every tribe and tongue and people and nation" (Rev. 5:9). This is the meaning of the Court of the Gentiles. Gentile (ethne) means tongue, tribe, people and nation. It means the nations. So, the people are standing in the Court of the Nations, waving palm branches, praising God for the completed harvest.

Everything about the Israelites had a missionary purpose — their law, their festivals, where they were located. The Israelites were given life and covenant for the nations, freedom as a testimony for the nations, the law as a witness to the nations, land for easy access to the nations, feasts for the celebration of the nations, discipline as a sign to the nations, captivity as an invasion of the nations and victory as a wonder to the nations.

Notes

1. Kingsley Fletcher, *Catch On Fire!* (Tulsa: Albury Publishing, 1984), p. 9.
2. C. Peter Wagner, Praying With Power Conference, Colorado Springs, CO, February 10, 1999.
3. Vinita Hampton and Carol Plueddemann, *World Shapers* (Wheaton: Harold Shaw Publishers, 1991), p. 9.

eleven

Sanctified Bigots

The opposite of love is not hate, it's indifference.
C. S. Lewis

"I am convinced that every person can be given the
compassionate **heart of God**. The **heart of God** is
for the people of the world."[1]
Bobbye Byerly

Riots

Like a flash, the mood of the crowd changed. Those who had been honoring Jesus
were now openly threatening murder! What could stir them up so quickly and so
deeply? We have seen this scene played out in our Bible movies . . . Jesus read
from the scroll of Isaiah and then announced the year of Jubilee. At that point, the
people became indignant and thought Jesus was blasphemous. When he made the
pronouncement, "Today this is fulfilled in your hearing," He was claiming to be
the long-awaited Messiah. So they went crazy, tearing their clothing and trying to
push him off the cliff like some primitive neighborhood vigilante group.

That is not how it happened. See Luke 4:22. Even after Jesus said these things, the
people admired Him. Everyone was pleasantly surprised by the beautiful words
that came out of Jesus' mouth. "Could this be Joseph and Mary's boy?" they asked
proudly. They liked Him saying he was the Messiah, because it was the greatest
thing that had ever happened to Nazareth, and besides, it might even be true. You
can almost see the Nazareth Times headlines reading, *"Home Town Boy Makes It
Big! Little Jesus is the Messiah!"*

No, what really drove them crazy was what Jesus said after He claimed to be the
Messiah. He pointedly went on to talk of God's love for all nations, not just Israel.
He spoke of God's desire to bless all the peoples of the earth through Israel, the
prophets and His Messiah. He ticked them off ("They were filled with wrath.")
when He started to point out that although there were plenty of starving, needy

widows in Israel, Elijah was sent to a foreign widow, and though there were many unhealed lepers in Israel, He chose to heal a political enemy of Israel, Naaman, the Syrian General. That is what did it. With deep hatred, the mob attacked Jesus, in an attempt to murder God's Messiah, because of the revelation that God was not only concerned about the nations, but that at times He prioritized the nations' blessing over Israel's!

I remember the first time I felt the gaze of this kind of mob. I was in college, and the church right next to the college campus was in the process of buying a big organ. Their promotional package (to get us all to give) actually claimed that with this organ:

> "We'll sing better! Yes we will!
> We'll worship better! Yes we will!"

Being one of the local missions radicals, I thought I needed to challenge the idea that it was okay to spend $78,000 dollars on this instrument, in light of the pressing needs of the world. It seemed like an opulent expenditure for our own selfish pleasures. Not to mention that it had a bit of pride attached to it. (The brochure handed out to the members of the church continued to say that this would then be the best organ in Idaho.) While this church had a stellar record of giving over ten percent of its total offerings to missions, the people somehow felt that this meant the rest of their money could be spent on whatever they fancied. They already had a very fine organ, but needless to say my challenge to their priorities was not welcomed. While millions die and go to hell, they wanted to sing prettily and were quite upset with my suggestion that God would not see it their way. They bought the new organ.

A Whale of a Story
Jonah is a miracle book. The fish is amazing; the people of Ninevah repenting is incredible, but the fact that the Book of Jonah is even in the Old Testament Canon is a complete wonder. The Jews hated the Ninevites. The Book of Jonah, tells the story of God's love for one of Israel's enemy peoples. At one time, the Ninevites had dominated Israel, capturing the northern territories. This was a political enemy, and yet God showed mercy, love and forgiveness toward them.

You might not remember who Jonah was. He was perhaps the greatest prophet of the Old Testament. Jonah, under Jeroboam the Second actually revived Israel and encouraged the worship of the One, True God. He encouraged Israel to go into battle against the Ninevites, and through Jonah's encouragement, Israel won back the northern territories. (2 Kings 14:25) There was a good reason that Jonah did not want to go to Ninevah. He was not a popular guy there. If we did not have the Book of Jonah, we would say that Jonah ranks as one of the greatest of the prophets in leading Israel in revival and military success.

But the story did not end there. God did call him to go to the Ninevites. The Ninevites were bad people. When God said it was time for them to be judged, He was right. God's judgments are correct every time. These were bloodthirsty people. They loved to "crucify" their captives on the outside of their wall around the city. They rejoiced in the screams of captives, as they slowly died on the wall. Worse, the Ninevites used to capture people who were in rebellion to them, and they would cut them around the belly and roll the skin up off their body, over their head and off their fingertips. They would totally denude their enemies of their upper torso. They would laugh at them and have them walk through the city streets until they collapsed and died. That was their fun. Did they deserve God's judgment? You better believe it. They were an evil generation, a nation in dark sin, and God sent Jonah there.

After hearing Jonah's preaching, all of Ninevah repented of their sin! This was the most successful, citywide evangelistic campaign ever launched! Billy Graham would have loved these results, but not Jonah. Jonah mumbled, "I knew you were going to forgive them. That's why I didn't want to come here." That is what he said. Sit down and read the whole book of Jonah. It is very fast reading. The last paragraph is a contrast between our concern and God's concern. Remember that Jonah was angry that God had saved the Ninevites, and he was angry that his little shelter dried up and withered away. God said, "You are so concerned about your comfort, your shelter. It is short-lived at best, and you did nothing to put it there." You can read it yourself — the last paragraph of Jonah. God continued, "Why then should I not be concerned about the 120,000 men who do not know their left hand from their right hand — who do not know right from wrong — who live in the city of Ninevah?"

Do you see the contrast between our concerns and God's concerns? Israel's concerns and God's concerns? Jonah's concerns and God's concerns? Are we are so concerned about our own homes, our own comforts, our own security, our own reputations, and not about the 120,000 in utter spiritual darkness who are justly judged to die, unless a preacher goes, and they turn from their sin and repent? Often the problem in our churches today is that we are so full of concern for our own comfort and desires that we have little concern for the Ninevites.

For God So Loved the Iraqis

I was browsing in a Christian bookstore when I came across a book entitled *The Islamic Invasion*. Its subtitle was something along the line of, "A look into the world's fastest growing religion." The cover had this alarmist appeal in an attempt to strike morbid fear into the heart of every red-blooded American.

The truth of the matter about Islam is great news! Islam is the world's fastest growing religion, **only after Christianity!** Jesus' kingdom is ever expanding, and Islam is no match. (True Christianity is growing at 6.9 percent growth rate[2], compared to 2.7 for Muslims, 2.3 percent for Hindus, and 1.7 percent for Buddhist.[3]) The last twenty years have seen more Iranians become Christians than the previous 1,000 years combined![4] Among the Muslim Fulanis in one African country, there is now a confirmed group of 60,000 (estimated to be closer to 100,000) converts to Christ![5] God is moving mightily among the Algerian Kabyles, a Berber people. There are now between 5,000 - 10,000 new believers. Now there is scarcely a Kabyle village without a believer![6]

Muslims worship Allah! There are those who would deny Allah as God, but He is undeniably the same Creator God who is holy and just, the Judge of all! Mohammed took the name "Allah" to identify God because the Syrian Christians with whom he stayed were using it (and had been for 600 years previously). This seems like a strange argument, especially when we use the term "Gott," (God) a German pagan deity that missionaries adopted and redefined. When talking to the Greeks, both the Jews and the Christians used the somewhat inadequate term "Theos." When speaking to a Muslim, you are speaking with a son of Abraham, having knowledge (though incomplete) of God, very similar to speaking to a Jew. In some ways, it is much easier to evangelize Muslims than Hindus or Tribals, where "which god?" becomes the question.

This is not an attempt to gloss over the difficulties of Muslim evangelism and conversion. Of all of the world's unreached peoples, the most untouched with the Gospel are the world's over 1 billion Muslims. But we must recognize that it is time for us to push past the myths that "the Arab world is unreachable" and the attitude that "God doesn't care for the Muslims."

It is time for the Church to recognize the Arab world as reachable and for the Muslims to rise to the top of our missions agenda. Presently, there is only one Christian missionary for every 1 million Muslims, and only 1/10 of every penny of every dollar given to the local church in North America goes to the Muslim world.[7] Bob Sjogren, the co-founder of Frontiers, a mission agency that deals entirely with evangelizing the Muslims, says that the key problem why so few Muslims as of yet have turned to Christ is simple, "If you sow little, you will reap little."[8]

The Church has a weak history of reaching out to the Muslims. In the Crusades, we waged bloody warfare, yet I cannot help but think that our current status of ignoring them is more cruel. The alarmist attitude is not Christian. It does little more than breed fear, which destroys any chance for Jesus' love to be expressed through us. Worse, it is faithless, making God out to be a liar. The Bible clearly states that His Kingdom is without end. (After the miracle of China, it is amazing that doubters still exist.) Our task will not be complete until we love the Muslims into the Kingdom.

We Hate Muslims

Or so it would seem. In 1991, during the Persian Gulf conflict, everyone began to don their yellow or orange ribbons to show their support of, and remember to pray for the Allied troops and the POW's. I began a green ribbon campaign. My wife and I began to wear green ribbons everyday. People would stop out of curiosity and ask what it represented. I would reply, "It is to remind us to pray for the thousands of Iraqi soldiers who are facing eternity never having a chance to hear of Jesus even once." Their faces would darken, and they would say, "Oh, that's interesting." Few were considering the Iraqis. Though some had family members in the conflict, and they were obviously concerned for their family members, the vast majority of us Americans were concerned about how the war was affecting our gasoline prices. We were not concerned about the Iraqis' eternal condition.

A good question to ask is this: Are we Americans or Christians first? We are no longer citizens of America when we become citizens of God's Kingdom. America is not our primary concern. Jesus and His Kingdom are. Should we have had the President's perspective on the event or King Jesus'? Should we have been cheering our smart bombs or weeping for the slain children of God? When we look at this war from His Kingdom perspective, what we see are people who have never heard of Jesus and have been locked in the lie of Islam for centuries and are about to go into eternity. 300,000 Muslims were sent to hell by our tax dollars, and we thought it was time to be proud. I am not saying what America should or should not have done. I am not pushing my political views here. I am saying that the Church did not care. The Iraqis were not a part of our prayer meetings or our broken hearts, as we saw people dying. Our bigotry against the Muslims was showing, and it still shows.

During the Iran Hostage Crisis in 1979, Greg Livingston, cofounder of the mission agency, Frontiers, was asked to come and speak at a famous and large church on the East Coast. After arriving there, he was informed that it was not the sermon that he was giving; it was "The Missions Minute!" Sitting there in that massive church with those thousands of people, he was begging God for help on what he should say. Finally the time came for "The Missions Minute," and he stood and asked: "How many of you are praying for the hostages in Iran?" All hands were raised. Then he asked, "How many of you are praying for the millions of Iranians held captive by the lie of Islam?" Only a few hands were raised. As the church became still in the horror of that question, he left the platform quietly saying, "I thought you were Christians, and this was a Christian church."[9]

One More Time

Peter's reputation for being thick-headed is well deserved. For him, God seemed to have to do things over and over again to make sure it got through, (i.e. "Do you love Me?") to the third power. In Acts, God had to thump him on the head three times before Peter would let go of his prejudices, traditions and nationalism, to obey God. To Peter's credit, he did obey, finally.

What was the deal with Peter? He had been filled with the Holy Spirit, baptized in power and boldness, graduated from Our Lord's Bible College (a three-year course) and yet still something was out of place. He could not seem to grasp that God loved the peoples of the world. He was stuck in a prejudiced position of thinking God's blessings, and Peter's ministry, were for the Israelites. With great force, Jesus pushed him beyond that narrow view, to begin ministering to the Gentiles.

Peter never fully got over His prejudice it seems. Later on, Paul had to openly rebuke Peter for his prejudicial bigotry. Perhaps God had a greater ministry to give to Peter, more like Paul's in scope and influence, had Peter been a more willing student. Many today consider sanctification, the empowerment of God, to be the ultimate experience, the goal line of Christianity, the end of all ends, yet clearly for Peter, it was not the end in itself; it was the first layer. He had another death and that was to His own cultural bigotry. As humans, this is tough. Many missionaries do not know the difference between their own preferences, traditions and cultures, so they impart a Gospel mixed with many unnecessary extras. (To see how the church resolved this issue, see Acts 15.)

We get all mixed up with our human nationalism and what God wants. Often we ignore the Bible's mandates, or adjust them to fit our paradigms. (After the many times Christ commanded them to take this Gospel to all the *ethne* (nations), Peter did not get it.) Even after Peter gave the great pronouncement of salvation for all nations in Acts 2, he still was not accepting it. God had to give him a vision three times (Acts 10:9-23) until finally he proclaimed with amazement: In truth I perceive that God shows no partiality. But in every nation whoever fears him and works righteousness is accepted by Him. (Acts 10:34-35)

Missionaries are Imperialists
Governments all over the world are hostile to missionaries. Missionaries are a "threat to the local culture and customs." Missionaries represent intolerance to established religions by claiming that Jesus is the only way. And, the missionaries are suffering from a misguided zeal for western culture and arrogant imperialism.

If you have noticed, Hollywood is quick to agree. How many movies have been made that spotlight the harmful effect missionaries in their "western imperialism" have had on native culture? Some are not exaggerations. Sadly, some missionaries have been more concerned with clothing the women and "civilizing the savages," than giving them the Good News of the Gospel in their own cultural context.

However, missionaries *are* to be imperialists, and so should you be. We are not capitalists, trying to sell the Gospel, nor are we industrialists trying to manufacture cookie cutter churches and their complex programs. We are proclaiming the Kingdom of God and the time for rebels to repent and submit. We in America are confused about God. God is not a Republican. He is not even pro-democracy. He is an absolute Monarch. He has supreme authority; He alone is sovereign. He is regal and majestic, our Emperor. In the Kingdom of our great and awesome God, there is only one government: Imperial rule!

"Imperial" comes from the Latin "imperium," which means command. When He asks of us, we give. When He commands us, we obey. There is not someone else's opinion to seek, nor a vote to be taken. He rules! The dividing line between those who are on the Emperor's side and those who are not is obedience to the command. Very simply, there is one command that we in America are having trouble obeying. It is the imperial command given from the King of Kings to extend the Empire's authority over every tongue, tribe and nation.

As I travel across America appealing to my brothers and sisters to lay down their lives in going and giving obedience to our Emperor's Great Commission, I see a people who have divided loyalties. Both are calling for obedience. The tendency is that most American Christians try to find a middle road between the two competing loyalties. Alas, the Christian walk is a narrow road, not a middle road. One pastor at a 4th of July service I attended even went so far as to try and marry these two competing loyalties. At the end of the service, the pastor gave an altar call to rededicate ourselves to "God and country."

On one hand the King asks Christians to lay down their lives and follow Him to the ends of the earth, but their inaction betrays the true government of their heart: the pursuit of happiness, the pursuit of property, the pursuit of prosperity — the American Dream. "Men do not reject the Bible because it contradicts itself but because it contradicts them."[10]

This is a crisis in our churches today. Test me on this . . . Drive by a church building with flags flying in front. Is it the imperial flag of Christ that flies highest, or is it the flag of our earthly home? As Leonard Ravenhill stated, "Old Glory or His Glory?"[11] Where does our loyalty lie? Until His Kingdom rule and its expansion becomes our top priority, with no competing loves, the Church in America will continue its course toward death, because you cannot have the best of both worlds. Your loyalty must be given to one Master or the other. Which flag flies higher over your church? Which flag flies highest in your life? The star spangled banner or the banner of Christ? I would that all of us could be called imperialists.

The Acid Test of Lordship

So much of the Church is running around like Jonah's and Peters, claiming the title of Prophet of God, yet not representing His desires for the nations. They are full of their own congregation's interests, or their community's, perhaps even their nation's, while showing no concern, and yes, even displaying occasional bigotry and hatred. Over time I have had several wild things said to me to try and excuse individuals from God's concern for the peoples of the world: "The black race isn't a descendent of Adam's race and, therefore, doesn't have original sin; so they are in no need of the Gospel." "We need to spend our time and money and personnel on the white race who Jesus died for . . ."

That may seem a bit extreme, but I run into that and other such nonsense that tries to diminish the imperative nature of Christ's command to "Go and make disciples of every tongue, tribe and nation." It may be a subtler form of disobedience disguised in pseudo logic, "There is so much to be done here," but it is the same at its root. Jesus is not their Lord. Comfort, home and race are their gods. In a day when I am convinced that there is no closed door that can keep the Gospel out, that there is no door shut to Jesus among the nations, I find that there is one door tightly shut: our hearts. Will He have the right to rule and reign in our lives, or will we limit Him to only a part?

Suppose there is a wedding, and when it is time for the vows the man says, "Pastor, I accept this woman as my personal cook, or as my personal dish washer." The woman would say, "Wait a minute. Yes, I'm going to cook. Yes, I'm going to wash dishes. Yes, I'm going to clean the house, but I'm not a maid. I'm going to be your wife. You have to give me your love, your heart, your home, your talent, everything." The same is true of Jesus. He is our Savior; He is our Healer, but we cannot cut Him into little pieces and take one part of Him and not another part of Him. When we take Him as our Savior, we are also taking Him as our Lord. When we ask Him for salvation, we accept His command to *"Go."*

Mario Murillo in his book *Fresh Fire* describes those who do not submit to the Lordship of Christ in every area as "high maintenance/low impact converts":

> They are born arrogant and weak. Imagine that combination! This breed is the product of the 1980's theological genetic engineering. They have never felt the sting of repentance and, therefore, have never experienced true resurrection. Since they are born with an inflated sense of self-importance, they interpret every scripture and define every experience from a "what can it do for me" attitude...They know of their biblical rights but none of their responsibilities. Their common bond is that they are users, not givers. They have no thirst for depth, no long-term commitment, no faith beyond feeling, and no sense of mission to a hurting world. The thought of denying self to grow and be equipped to touch others is like quantum physics.[12]

The Acid Test of Lordship is the Great Commission.

It is here that the practical counting of the cost must be measured and paid to go and give up all, or to stay and give up all. Only until we place ourselves unreservedly at His disposal for His purposes on planet earth can we say Jesus is Lord. Watch out for teachers who preach all manner of insight, yet have no passion for the ends of the earth. When they say that it is "just not their ministry," they are people who have not seen the heart of God and who are not committed to the complete Lordship of Christ.

We all need to place ourselves under the Blood of Jesus when we seek salvation. We do not need to see our personal name in scripture; it is a general command that people everywhere repent and believe. The Great Commission of Jesus is just the same. The general command is there. We all must submit ourselves to the command of Christ and His great love for all peoples. Our name is in the Great Commission, if we consider ourselves as being under His authority. Our Name is in the Abrahamic Covenant to bless all peoples, if we are His children by faith. Until we surrender to His Commission to *"Go,"* we have not surrendered. We have no security of ever discovering His unique and perfect plan for our lives until we unreservedly, in light of His passion for every tongue, tribe, people and nation, say, "Lord, what do you want me to do? Do you want me to go?"

Jonah did not understand God's heart for all nations and found himself as whale vomit. If we are not aligned with His love for all peoples, we may find ourselves spit out. Judas was not pleased with Jesus' non-patriotic stance and ended up betraying Christ to death for some profit. Bigots and clueless ones, those who are out of step with what God is doing and what His great heart is about, often try to kill the messenger of that truth. We may find ourselves as part of the mob gladly trying to push Jesus and His message of love for all peoples over the cliff, or when He demands to be our King, we may in one voice scream "Crucify Him!"

Notes

1. "To the Ends of the Earth," (Christian Broadcasting Network, Inc., 1996).
2. Statistics from Strategic Frontiers YWAM, Colorado Springs, CO. Many of their Statistics are available online at http://www.sfcos.org.
3. Edythe Draper, *The Almanac of the Christian World* (Wheaton: Tyndale House Publishers, Inc., 1990), p. 81.
4. Ibid., p. 705.
5. Strategic Frontiers YWAM sources.
6. Strategic Frontiers YWAM sources.
7. Bob Sjogren, Co-founder of Frontiers, while speaking at a Perspectives On the World Christian Movement course in Oklahoma City, OK, 1996. Also www.gospelcom.net/awm.
8. Ibid.
9. Ibid.
10. Frank S. Mead, *Encyclopedia of Religious Quotations* (London: Peter Davies, Ltd., 1965), p. 26.
11. David Smithers, www.watchword.org, relates this as something said often to the young men who would gather at the Leonard Ravenhill home in Texas for prayer and discipleship.
12. Mario Marillo, *Fresh Fire* (Anthony Douglas Pub, 1991).

twelve

After God's Heart

"Any tear shed in sharing the **heartbeat of God**, any tear shed
through Christlike loving empathy with our fellowmen, any tear
born of the yearning constraint of the Holy Spirit is a tear by
which we serve the Lord. Nothing pleases Christ more than for
us to share with Him His burden for the world and its people.
Nothing so weds us to the **heart of Christ** as our tears shed as
we intercede for lost ones with Him. Then truly we become
people after **God's own heart**. Then we begin to know what it
is to be Christ's prayer partners."[1]
Wesley L. Duewel

"Let my heart be broken by the things
that break the **heart of God**."[2]
Bob Pierce

Steak Smothered in Hot Fudge Gravy.
Churches Growing Out of Control! Government issues stern warning to all
churches to obey city fire ordinances in conjunction with crowded buildings far
exceeding fire codes! The nets are so full they are starting to break!

Then we all wake up.

This scenario is not happening in the US. Maybe in China. Maybe in Central
America. But not here, at least not today, and here is the reason why. We have
been seduced by a cult. In every denomination this cult has been growing.

Much of the Gospel of Jesus Christ seems like a bitter pill, and we see a trend in
our churches to create a more palatable gospel. Increasingly the message seems to
be: "God is good for you. He makes your life happier and more fulfilling." True,
yet inadvertently we are feeding the self-preserving desire to be more comfortable,
which runs diametrically opposite to Christ's call to self-denial and service.

87

After God's Heart

All of us desire freedom from sacrifice and the strain and pain it brings. We all have the common fantasy of utopia on earth, a leftover echo from the Garden of Eden. Yet it is not until eternity that Jesus promises to wipe every tear from our eyes. It is now that He asks us to weep with Him, as He wept with a heart of compassion at the tomb of His good friend, Lazarus. How much more bitter are the tears He shed over those who knew Him not. We see our example, the Lord, crying painful tears over Jerusalem who rejected Him. In the same way, He wants us to weep over those who are lost. God still desires a companion who will share His heart's ache for the unreached and dying peoples of the world.

There are those who react adversely to the uncompromising message of sacrifice for the sake of those who are unevangelized. Those who call the Church into obedience to the Great Commission are accused of pulling on emotional strings and making people feel guilty. Somehow, we wrongly have in our thinking that Christ came only to give us emotions on the positive side of the spectrum. The implication being that it is a satanic action if our "peaceful utopia" is troubled. It is as if this generation only recognizes a gospel of fun and pleasure, a gospel that seeks to make people feel good and laugh heartily. We even have churches that make the "package" fun and entertaining. Preachers are now charged to give short "sermonettes" for the lukewarm "Christianettes."[3] Already, conviction is not acceptable in the Church. If we leave a service with anything but an emotional upper for a message, then the preacher is full of "condemnation and judgment." Those who seek their own pleasure will only find ruin! The end of this sugarcoated, syrup-covered cult gospel is the broad road of comfort and ease that leads to destruction.

Jesus exhorts us, "Blessed are you who weep and sob now for you will laugh" (Luke 6:21). He understood what the Psalmist wrote in Psalm 126:5-6, "He who continually goes forth weeping, carrying his bag of seed, shall indeed come again with a shout of joy, bringing his sheaves with him." But today's, pleasure-obsessed Christianity goes forth with joy and hardly notices that there is no harvest. So we pat each other on the back, encouraging each other to feel good about our ministries. Paul also knew this lost truth of "church growth." We must deny our comfort, our emotional easy chair and travail in "serving the Lord with all humility, and with many tears" (Acts 20:19).

In our stubborn refusal to enter into God's emotions for the lost, and in our disobedience to intercede, we have yet to grasp the sober seriousness and eternal issue at stake. We have two choices. Either we beg while on earth, or the lost will beg in Hell, as did the rich man in Luke 16. If we do not weep now, they will weep then. If we do not embrace our momentary light affliction on their behalf now, then they will be engulfed by eternal affliction.

After God's Own Heart

> The Lord has sought for Himself **a man after His own heart**, and the Lord has appointed him as ruler over His people . . . (1 Sam. 13:14).

There is only one man in the Bible who is called a "man after God's own heart." What was it about this shepherd boy that became king that would give him such honor? What set apart the life of this music playin', giant slayin', spear dodgin', cave hidin', psalm writin' youngest son of Jesse? Charles Swindoll in his Bible study on David states that this title is such that "we might think of him as some kind of spiritual Superman in a world without a trace of kryptonite. But he wasn't studded with superhuman qualities. God doesn't select his servants on the basis of Atlas physiques or Einstein intellects."[4]

David was one who was abandoned to his God. This was a man of great stature and responsibility, yet he still danced about wildly before the ark of his God! He was a man who knew of God's desire to be known throughout the earth, and desired to do everything He could to bring Him the honor due Jehovah's Name.

How did this shepherd boy grow to be the man who would be called "after My own Heart?" How did this fugitive gain the rank of the throne of David, which shall never end, which Christ will sit upon and bring justice to the nations? David was indeed a man after God's own heart. He reflected God's heart, and He pursued God's heart.

How do you become Christlike? You pursue the things in which Christ is interested. You begin to pursue His heart, His interests, what is on His mind, and you cannot help but begin reflecting what He is interested in, what He is concerned about, His attitudes. David was a man like this. He was not the perfect man, but he was somebody pursuing God's heart.

This pursuit can be seen in two ways. First, he was completely in love with God. It is hard to think of a man being more attached to His Creator. The Psalms have a way of lifting our worship of God into realms only briefly considered. This is a degree of intimacy that is missing from many churches, having been replaced by a cold formalism. Not many in our pews would consider dancing in wild abandonment before the Lord, but David did. (2 Sam. 6:20)

The second issue we see all the way through the Psalms is David's singing of God's purpose to make Himself known to all nations. Psalms is crowded with understanding of God's global intent. Psalm 1 is passion for God, and Psalm 2 is God being King of the Nations and understanding His purposes among the nations. Let us look at Psalm 96:1-3:

Oh sing to the Lord a new song! Sing to the Lord all the earth. Sing to the Lord, bless His Name; Proclaim the goodness of His salvation from day to day. Declare His glory among the nations, His wonders among all peoples.

This new song has to do with God's glory among the peoples, His salvation among the nations. "Declare it, Israel!"

Psalms is full of God's heart for the nations. We do not have space here to go through the whole book, but pay attention as you are reading the Psalms. It may get a bit irritating from now on. Every time you look at them, in fact, every time you look at your Bible from now on, you will have trouble not seeing the nations there.

When people die, it is important to pay attention to their last words. David's last Psalm before He died was Psalm 72:

Blessed be the Lord God, the God of Israel, Who only does wondrous things! And blessed be His name forever! And **let the whole earth be filled with His glory.** Amen and Amen. The prayers of David the son of Jesse are ended (Ps. 72:18-20).

I am convinced this is God's favorite verse. "May the knowledge of the glory of the Lord cover the earth as the waters cover the sea." It is repeated at least fourteen times in scripture. It is as though He cannot wait for another generation to pass, so that He can say it again through another one of His prophets. "May the whole earth know the glory of the knowledge of the Lord."

David perfectly understood God's heart. Though Muslims believe that God is unknowable, He desires to be known — He reveals Himself — the hallmark of a Christian is one who knows his God.

God speaks only to those who take time to listen. It is the man who cares who communes with the Most High and learns the secrets of the Lord. Such a man also sees the sorrow and feels the woe of the world. He shares the burdens of his brothers.[5]

Bride of Christ

While at a family reunion, a great uncle of my wife's came up with tears in his eyes exclaiming, "The young people, they just don't understand intimacy with Jesus." He was wrought with sorrow, as he looked at the younger generations pursuing the world and denying Christ. He went on, "When I was in the army about to cross over the Rhine into Germany, I was scared. I prayed, "God, I don't know if you've got any use for me, but I just want you to know that if I survive,

I'm yours to do with as you please.'" Turning to me and looking at me with eyes full of tears, he blurted out, "For forty years I have been faithful and He has never failed me."

My wife's uncle knew one missing element in these young folks' lives. It was *fidelity* to Jesus. Much of our parents' and grandparents' commitment to Jesus had to do with fidelity, kind of like their marriages. When they got married, they were getting in for life. Divorce was not talked about; it was never an option.

This commitment to fidelity is vital! Even if things go terribly, they made a commitment, and they will stick by it. Even if the romance and feelings are gone, they will stay married until their death. However, I would call this a passionless marriage. It leads to terrible boredom. Many of our churches are like that. Passionless. Our kids are bored and leaving, as soon as they can. The older folks are committed to Christ, but it has been quite some time since they felt like David did, wanting to twirl before God, dancing and shouting.

I remember as a boy climbing the stairs of my grandparents' house in Sacramento and peering into their room. The old furniture, the wallpaper, and the two beds. I never understood that whole two-bed thing. Maybe if one moved around too much, or something, I could see it . . . nah. I think much of the subsequent generation felt the same way I did. We knew that passion was valuable. The hippie movement was born of this sympathy, "If it feels good, do it." That generation's pursuit of emotional passion led to such brilliance as "If you're not with the one you love, love the one you're with." And a whole generation abandoned fidelity for *passion*.

In the Church, I see whole denominations formed out of the hippies and yuppies (both born out of self-gratification, one based in a counter-culture, the other in an ultra pro-culture). The Charismatic movement in many ways can be understood in the light of people coming out of fidelity only, boring churches, knowing that there must be more of God to be had, experiencing the joy of worship and the release of the Spirit to dance before Him.

I was standing in a citywide praise and worship gathering, when I noticed the man in front of me energetically worshiping God with His hands raised. When the song ended, he immediately began to eye the girl in front of him with all the classic signs of lust. I believe, in a nutshell, he is the fruit of "passion only" churches. In their pursuit of feeling God, they have made "feeling" their God. Whatever feels good will be my pursuit. Whomever I am with, I will love.

Now, before you who are more of the fidelity persuasion get all "I told you so-ish," know that your lack of passionate intimacy with Jesus is pushing your kids to seek from the world what only Jesus can give. Our churches are in decline in

America. We are not even maintaining biological growth, because our people are bored — and children are only born from a common bed of intimacy. We need more than head nods to our spouse, Jesus; we need closeness.

A church that does not know how to worship and let God touch the core of the worshiper's heart is questionable in its gospel. Never forget that Jesus tells us through the conversation with the woman at the well, that God seeks worshipers in spirit and truth. Many of us focus on truth, and do not know of what spirit we are. When all of time is ended and the missionary task is over and we stand before the Lamb, only one thing will remain to be done. It will not be evangelism; it will not be preaching; it will not even be Bible study; it will be worship.

On the other side, churches who think that if only people could experience God once, they would change, and yet never preach repentance, and holiness, let me address you. One pastor friend of mine repeatedly warned me to stop using terms such as "rebellion" and "sin" when talking about his people. They were not "stiff necked;" they were misled. They were not sinful; they were "deceived." I guess when it comes right down to it they were not needing the death of Jesus and His blood for the forgiveness of sin, they were needing a hug because they were having a bad day.

At this same family reunion, was a young man who all day played on the lake. He had a real lust problem with the women. I kept my wife well covered and far from his leering eyes. I was not given a word of knowledge about his sin; it was just obvious. That evening he slipped on a Promise Keepers[a] shirt and proceeded to lead us in worship. He needed a good dose of old-fashioned holiness preaching. Our churches will always be immature and a reproach to the Gospel, if we do not marry *fidelity* and *passion* and get past the satanic division.

Compatibility

When these first two, fidelity and passion, are in place, God desires to bring forth the type of marriage He seeks. When I married my wife, it was not just because I was physically attracted and emotionally infatuated, nor was it just an intellectual, logical commitment that I was making. I also loved being with her. We liked to do things together.

This is the third component that God is looking for in this mystery of the Church and Christ, the Bride and the Bridegroom. Jesus wants a compatible wife, not just a passionate one, not just a committed one, but a compatible Bride, One who likes what He likes, One who wants to go where He likes to go.

Somehow we think He wants a prissy woman who spends hours teasing her hair and playing with her makeup getting perfectly spotless, buying new clothes and shoes, when what He wants is a Bride who will touch the lepers and walk the dusty trails. This explains why so many churches are spending time and energy on their own beautification or purity, and only the religiously expected amount for the unreached. The admonition is "Be ye not unequally yoked." Jesus will not go against His own Word. He will surely not be unequally yoked. He will not marry a girl who is not committed to Him even unto death. Nor will He marry a girl who is not in love with Him. Most alarmingly, He will not be yoked to someone who is not in line with His self-sacrificing passion for every tongue, tribe and nation.

I have thought of how to be acceptable in this department, but some will just have to not like me for a minute while I finish this out. The picture of marriage is the yoking of two oxen together to pull a plow in the same direction. However, if the oxen are going in opposite directions, yoking them together will only bring disaster. If our churches and the people within them are focused on their own comforts and the building of their own kingdoms, Christ cannot be yoked with them. If we are sold out to money and security, we are serving mammon and the flesh; Christ is not our Master, and we are not yoked with Him. (Amos 3:3)

Until we reach compatibility with Him and His purposes, we will never truly be one with our Husband. This is what Jesus was doing when He approached Peter three times in the vision. Peter's fidelity had been resolved. His passion for Jesus was well documented. What was lacking? It was not the Holy Spirit's power. It was not His cleansing. It was the Holy Spirit's heart, His purposes on the earth in which the Husband wanted Peter to partner. Beyond commitment and filling of the Spirit is this place of intimacy called compatibility.

Hearing His Heartbeat
In the picture of the Last Supper, we see John resting his head on the breast of Jesus. This is a picture of intimacy. He is listening to the beating of that great Heart. It is a picture meant for His Bride, the Church. We must be close enough to Him to hear His concerns, dreams and desires. It is in the place of intimate communion that we discover what makes Jesus tick, and begin to enter into a oneness that is the mystery of this eternal marriage. (Amos 3:7)

As we resolve not to turn away from His emotions and begin to pursue the things that are on His heart, we will inevitably encounter The 10/40 Window. The 10/40 Window is where the vast majority of the world's unreached people groups live. This geographical area is located between 10 degrees by 40 degrees N. latitude, stretching from the deserts of North Africa over to the islands of Indonesia and up into what used to be Soviet Central Asia. It is like a black hole in the blessing that God promised through Abraham and his descendants. If we are the light of the world, this is where it is dark.

Materially speaking, this is where the poorest of the poor live. When our poor are hungry, they have places to go for help. The poor in The 10/40 Window have no place to go, and millions die of starvation in these areas. This is where the worst of the worst problems are. When you think of the starving children with bloated stomachs, this is where they are.

When you think of the oppressive governments in the world, you think of Tienanmen Square. You think of the human rights violations in Myanmar or the killing fields of Cambodia. You think of Iraq and its gassing and torture of the Kurds to the north and the Shiites to the south. They are here in this Window. Corruption abounds, and governments seem to have permission to do whatever they will with their people.

When considering natural disasters, they take the worst toll in this area. Perhaps you remember when Hurricane Andrew smashed into Florida. It was a horrible thing — billions of dollars of damage and 58 deaths. We sent water bottles and truckloads of food. The newspapers were full of the accounts. America's minds and attentions were focused there. That very same week a cyclone, which is the same thing as a hurricane, smashed into Bangladesh. I found it on page seven of the Daily Oklahoman on the day it hit. 135,000 people in Bangladesh died in that storm. We cannot comprehend that number. It was on page seven, and the churches were not called to mourning and weeping and prayer for the lost. We were concerned about our property.

I can hear the discussion between God and Jonah all over again: *"You're concerned about your property and your comfort, and it is short lived at best. Why shouldn't I be concerned about the 135,000 people?"* They were swept out to sea without ever having heard of Jesus Christ, not having a chance like you and I have from our childhood to repent and mess up and repent again. Nothing! They went into eternity, into that darkness, without having heard the Name of Jesus Christ. We treated them like animals, as if they did not have souls.

Actually, we did not treat them as animals, did we? If 135,000 monkeys had been swept out to sea, we would have been up in arms. Two whales get stuck in ice, and we are concerned. A dog is stuck in a hole somewhere, and we are concerned. 135,000 people for whom Jesus bled, died, cared, and loved were swept out to sea without us acknowledging them.

This is The 10/40 Window. 95% of all the unreached peoples of the world are locked into the demonic stronghold of The 10/40 Window. Peoples without Jesus are imprisoned behind the high walls of Animism and Hinduism, Chinese idolatry, Buddhist hopelessness and Islam's laws. Some of the most demonic religions are in The 10/40 Window. Tibetan Buddhism is one example. Hollywood makes it look like a peaceful ideology, but it is a lie. I have been to Mongolian and Tibetan villages long held captive by this Llhamastic Buddhism. The people are struggling under terrible oppression and fear. In one Tibetan temple, I saw the most demonic idol I have ever encountered. The god that they worship is crushing people under his claw-like feet. It has skulls for the hair, blood streaming out of his mouth, as he is chewing on people, while raping a woman. This is their god. And Hollywood is putting out movies that make Tibetan Buddhism appear to have some good philosophies. Do not believe it! I have seen it! It is oppressive and demonic. They actually have incantations that help the Llamas levitate off the ground while rolling hot coals over their tongue, invoking demonic spirits to curse their enemies.

The people whom Satan has locked in Tibetan Buddhism have been locked in it for thousands of years without the freedom of Jesus Christ. We have walked in that freedom for how many years? Our people have been free for hundreds of years, and these unreached peoples are still locked in bondage. I will not be happy if I die and their condition is unchanged. How many generations have to go by without something changing? Sitting at home and wishing is not going to make a change. It will change by our being brave men and women of God, stepping out, and giving up our shopping malls. We must give up our culture, our comfort and our friends, and like Abraham follow God to the land He will show us. It takes brave, war-like actions, violent actions, laying it all down for the sake of Jesus Christ and His Kingdom. He is worth it, friends! Those missionaries, who threw their lives into Africa with their coffins in tow, knew that the Lamb was worthy of that price.

I Lost My Crown
A few years ago I wept like a baby. It should have been the best of news, but all it brought me was intense grief and a deep heart pain. I had just received a letter from a missionary in Taiwan letting me know that two dear friends had become Christians. Jamie and I had lived with this family for over a year and had desired to see them brought to Jesus. He was the eldest son of a Taiwanese family and she the eldest daughter of a Hakka family, both groups unreached with the Gospel. After years of visiting, praying and working, they knew Jesus! But I was lost in a world of emotional pain. Friends tried to comfort me and I myself, with the words, "It must be because you were not there to bring them in yourself, to be the one to reap," or "You're concerned for their discipleship." I agree that both were desires and concerns . . . but that was not my pain.

A year went by, and my spirit had a dead spot in it. Finally, it was brought to life, and as though no time had passed, I found myself in the same mess of deep pain and weeping. I was heart broken, and this time I knew why. I had missed my crown.

Is that not the silliest thing you have ever heard of? I never enjoyed those southern gospel songs about rewards and crowns with jewels, but this crown is not an object to set uncomfortably on my head. It is a gift of God, an outpouring of joy and pleasure that Paul knew when he said to the Thessalonians, "You are my glory" (1 Thes. 2:19-20). In an instant, I knew I had missed mine. No one can steal it. It was not taken . . . I had, of all horrible things, forfeited my glory.

I have always known what it would take to bring Liou Jin Hwa and Ming Shwe into the Kingdom. But, when I was there, I pursued my own pleasure and satisfaction and never, but in a very painless way, laid down my life for them. I know my heart, and I did not! So the years went by — years that they served their demonic idols, teaching their children to worship those vile things, years that were to be in service of Jesus — were it not for my damnable selfishness and unfaithfulness to Jesus. What pain I caused Him. What pain I caused them.

Now I share the punishment for disobedience and the anguish He felt for them, and I feel the hole where my reward should be. Oh, how the unreached fall like a waterfall into eternity without Jesus, and oh, how we daily refuse to die for them. For my friends, it just prolonged their agony, but for most, it is their doom.

There is a crown, a glory that God has set aside for us in the Church. It is a glory that He would share with us, yet we can forfeit this glory. It is a joy that will fill our lives or a shame that will pierce our soul. I know what it is, and so do you, my dear friend and reader. Now is not the time for casual pursuit of the lost, but it is time to dive in with headlong abandon. Now is the time for the Church to fall on her face before the Righteous Judge and plead for the lives of those lost in The 10/40 Window. It is time for us, the Body of Christ, to die again.

Let your hearts be crushed by the lost in the world. Let your light-heartedness be smitten with a picture of eternity. May their death be as your own, for only then can their salvation be your joy and their life be your glory. It is not clever technology that will see salvation brought to the ends of the earth. It is the taking on of His Name, His nature and character, the living of His life and the partaking in His sufferings and death.

> For the eyes of the Lord move to and fro throughout the
> earth that He may strongly support those whose heart is
> completely His (2 Chron. 16:9a).

As we find ourselves pursuing His heart and beginning to be burdened by His cares and concerns, God will strongly support us. Phillips Brooks correctly states, "I do not pray for a lighter load, but for a stronger back."[6] When God looks at your life in His search across the earth, does He find in you a heart that is fully His? Being one who is after God's own heart means a unique blending with Him. Even as a married couple shares each other's debts, sorrows and joys, so we begin to be burdened by His cares.

Song of Love

James Hudson Taylor, great missionary to China, only wrote two books in his lifetime.[7] The first was, in essence, his declaration of war on the kingdom of darkness in China. This first book launched the China Inland Mission. The second was written at the height of his fame. What do you think this missionary had to say? What would be his burning message to deliver to the Church? It was a commentary, a little guide, a study of his favorite book: The Song of Solomon. Why was this his favorite? He said that it "knit his heart to his Beloved."

Oh, what a sweet book of union with Jesus this Song of Solomon is. It is a picture of the Bridegroom and the Bride. The Bridegroom beckons His Beloved in chapter 4 verse 6 to run with Him on the "mountain of frankincense and myrrh." To our normal, North American mindset, perhaps that is a very romantic passage, but in reality there is nothing romantic about frankincense and myrrh. We interpret it as "Run with me on the perfumed mountains," but this is not what He is saying. Myrrh was used as an embalming spice. It was used for burial. Frankincense, then, was used by the priests when they were performing the blood sacrifices. They would add frankincense to the offering to help sweeten the smell of the burning flesh. It produced a fragrant offering. So, how romantic is it? Jesus beckons to His Beloved, *"Come run with me on the mountain of embalming, death and sacrifice."* This is indeed what Jesus has done with His Bride. He has asked us to follow Him in sacrifice and laying down our lives.

We see Jesus' desire for union with His Beloved, the Church. Revelation promises that someday the Bride will indeed be one with the Spirit of Christ:

The Spirit and the Bride say, "Come!" (Rev. 22:17)

Together they beckon the non-Christians of the world to come and drink of the water that is free. If anyone is thirsty, he or she can come and drink and be satisfied with the water of life! G. D. Watson states, "Thus we see, the Bridehood of the saints are preeminently of a missionary spirit, and share the very desires of Christ in urging people to come and drink of the pure, sweet water of Life."[8]

By the end of the Song of Solomon, most scholars agree that it is very difficult to determine who is speaking, the Bridegroom or the Beloved. Their voices become so entwined that we are unable to separate them. They are one. They have become united in speaking of their love for one another and their common commission and calling.

This is what happens in Revelation. The voice of the Spirit of Christ and the voice of the Bride have become one, and together in unity they say, "Come!"

Sing a song of celebration, lift up a shout of praise
For the Bridegroom will come, the Glorious One
And oh, we will look on His face.
We'll go to a much better place.

Dance with all your might!
Lift up your hands and clap for joy!
The time's drawing near, when He will appear,
And oh, we will stand by His side
A strong, pure, spotless Bride.

We will dance on the streets that are golden,
The glorious Bride and the great Son of Man,
From every tongue and tribe and nation,
We'll join in the song of the Lamb!

Sing aloud for the time of rejoicing is near.
The risen King, our Groom, is soon to appear.
The wedding feast to come is now near at hand.
Lift up your voice, proclaim the coming Lamb![9]

Notes

a. This is not an accusation against Promise Keepers -- just a story about someone that used their easy-to-get, merchandised shirts.

1. Wesley L. Duewel, *Ablaze For God* (Grand Rapids: Francis Asbury Press, 1989), p. 240.

2. Ruth Tucker, *From Jerusalem to Irian Jaya,* (Grand Rapids: Zondervan Publishing House, 1983), p. 468.

3. David Wilkerson, "The Solomon Church," Dec. 1994.

4. Charles Swindoll, *David, A Man After God's Own Heart* (Fullerton, CA: Insight For Living, 1988), p. 1.

5. Anita M. Bailey, quoted by A.W. Tozer, *God Tells the Man Who Cares* (Camp Hill, PA: Christian Publications, 1992), p. 1.

6. Frank S. Mead, *Encyclopedia of Religious Quotations* (London: Peter Davies, Ltd., 1965), p. 41.

7. *A Retrospect* -- J. Hudson Taylor's autobiography was actually a collection of articles he wrote for publication in China Inland Mission's magazine, "China's Millions."

8. George D. Watson, *The Bridehood Saints* (Cincinnati: God's Revivalist Press, 1880's) p. 39.

9. David Ruis, "We Will Dance," (Mercy Publishing, 1993)

thirteen

The Last Temptation of Christ

"Jesus was moved with compassion concerning the miseries of men. He saw them as lost, hungry, sick and bewildered. And just as His **Father's heart** had been moved in love to send Christ into the world to redeem them, so our Lord's own heart was moved in compassion toward them."[1]
G. Christian Weiss

"Is it possible to get close to the **Master's heart** without getting close to the Master's mission?"[2]
Larry Moyer

All the Kingdoms of the Earth

Matthew 4 contains the story of Satan tempting Jesus out in the desert. For the last great temptation, Satan took Jesus up to a tall mountain and showed him all the kingdoms and nations of the world and their glory. Satan dangled them in front of Jesus and said, "If you worship me, I'll give them to you."

Scripture is very clear. You cannot be tempted by something that you do not desire. (Jam. 1:14) Here was Satan's last great temptation of Jesus. I think I know what was going on in Jesus' mind. He was thinking, *"When I was in heaven, Lucifer, I used to look at you, the most glorious of my creation, and you were such a beautiful worship leader. Sometimes I just had this urge. I can't exactly explain it. I just wanted to slip off my throne and fall at your feet and worship you."* Was that the temptation? No, of course not! What was the temptation there on that mountain? All the kingdoms and their glory. All the peoples and nations of planet earth. The very reason that Jesus had left His throne in heaven and come to earth was to redeem people from every tongue, tribe and nation, and here Satan was giving Him a short cut to it. It was what He desired. This desire for the nations was the very core reason for His life. He desired it deeply enough that it could tempt God Almighty. Think of it.

I'll See Your Three and Up the Ante

The Pharisees were quite insightful and prophetic when they looked at Jesus and said, *"Look, the world has gone after Him" (John 12:19).* Indeed the world was beginning to go after Him. The very next verse we see some Greeks seeking an audience with Jesus. His fame and ministry were on the verge of going international. The very focus of His ministry was beginning to respond, when Jesus stepped back from the brink of fame once again.

Almost rudely, He ignored the Greeks and began talking about how a grain of wheat must die if it will bear much fruit. Jesus knew something no one else seemed to comprehend. He was born to die. Unless He died, He would remain alone, but if He died He would be multiplied through the lives of those who would follow. With Greeks knocking at His door, and all the other demands that would be made on Him to go there, come here, do this, speak to us . . . He must multiply Himself.

If it was only about discipleship mathematics, we could understand it, but another cosmic battle was going on — a war over the Kingdoms of this earth which the Prince of this World, Lucifer, had seized. Jesus was about to strike a fatal blow to His old enemy, the dragon, by running headlong into Satan's fiercest weapon: death.

> Now judgment is upon this world; now the ruler of this world
> will be cast out. And I, if I be lifted up from the earth, will draw
> all men to Myself (John 12:31-32).

In that terrifying death, Jesus, in one fell swoop, destroyed His enemy and tempter, and provided the very blessing the Greeks and all nations needed. He became the Lamb of sacrifice that fends off the Angel of Death.

When Satan had Jesus up on that tall mountain to offer Him the Kingdoms of the world, the plan had already been plotted in heaven how best to rescue the peoples of the earth and destroy the power of the evil one. It was a two-fold problem that God faced. One was rebellion. The other was sin. It might seem that they are the same problem at first glance. But rebellion was started in the heavenlies, and must be ultimately crushed. Sin also must be put out of the presence of God.

Satan infected man with this disease of sin, and unless God somehow could find an antidote for man's sin, then the fellowship that God desired would forever be denied Him.

Somehow He must preserve man that He loves, those who will look to His cure even as some looked at Moses' bronze snake that was lifted up in the wilderness and were healed. Likewise, He said "If I be lifted up . . ."

Jesus was, in a single action, fulfilling the Abrahamic covenant by providing Himself as the Lamb of sacrifice needed for the blessing of all peoples. At the same time, as the Lion of Judah, He was crushing the power of the rebellion, and establishing His Kingdom, which will never end.

Jesus' Joy

I was reading an old, crumbling book from the 1870's when I ran across this interesting story:

> Walking one day along the seashore, I saw a number of people running to the water's edge, and a boat putting off in haste. It was after a youth who, in bathing, had gotten out of his depth and sunk. After remaining for a quarter of an hour under water, he was taken out, and restoratives promptly applied to rekindle, if possible, the spark of life. I waited with many more at the door of the building to ascertain whether he was likely to recover. Several came out, but to tell of no hope. At length a person darted out of the house, the bearer of better tidings, "He has drawn a breath! He has drawn a breath!" The crowd caught and quickly echoed the cry. I thought of the joy that is felt in heaven when a penitent sinner is seen crying for mercy.[3]

In Luke 10, we see this heavenly joy in the life of Jesus. Here, He is as happy as any place in scripture. Yes, He was acquainted with grief, and a man of sorrows, but He was also a man anointed with the oil of gladness and joy! (Hebrews1:9) Jesus had just sent the seventy disciples out on their short-term missions trip into the surrounding villages. Many commentators agree that this was the evangelistic follow-up to the events surrounding the woman at the well. Jesus purposely had dragged His Jewish group into this Samaritan village, where he plopped down by a well for a rest, while they all went off looking for food (Probably what took them so long was that there was not a kosher-friendly store anywhere nearby.). A Samaritan woman came out to the well and ended up being the evangelist for her entire village.

Upon the disciples' return, Jesus then launched into a sermon on the harvest:

> Do you not say, "There are yet four months, and then comes the harvest?" Behold, I say to you, lift up your eyes, and look on the fields, that they are white for harvest (John 4:35).

103

As He was saying this to His Jewish disciples, the Samaritans began coming out to find out about the Man who told her everything she had ever done. As they lifted their eyes to see the harvest, what should greet them but a bunch of Samaritans, rarely considered higher than dogs by Jews, but worth everything to the heart of God. Jesus is basically saying, *"Go get 'em, boys."* He continues His speech in Luke 10:

> And He was saying to them, "The harvest is plentiful, but the laborers are few; therefore beseech the Lord of the harvest to send out laborers into His harvest" (Luke 10:2).

Jesus then told His seventy disciples to go out two by two to all the surrounding villages, giving them the same instructions we read in Matthew 10. The significant differences between these two passages are not in the instructions, but in who was sent and to whom. In Matthew 10, we see Jesus sending out the twelve to go only to the lost sheep of Israel, not to enter any Samaritan or Gentile city. Twelve is always the number reserved for Israel, or those who are Abraham's descendants. Twelve tribes, twelve disciples, etc. Notice that when Jesus is among the Samaritans, He sends out seventy? This is classically the number that represents the nations and languages of the earth. It comes from Genesis 10 where the peoples who come out of the Tower of Babel are listed. Yes, there are seventy. (If you are confused, it is because you are using the NIV, which thanks to the Septuagint uses the number 72. No matter, it is consistent in Genesis 10 and Luke 10.)

For many of the seventy, it was their first taste of cross-cultural evangelism. With this first proclamation of God's Kingdom in these Samaritan villages and the ensuing power encounters, Jesus' joy is so clearly understood. When the disciples returned, thrilled that the demonic powers obeyed them, Jesus got an odd look in His eyes. He either remembered back to a time before time, or looked to a future that was being affected by their activity of evangelism, and said, "I saw Satan fall like lightning from the sky." Then, after he warns them not to get all messed up, confusing powerful works with their salvation, He starts to get excited.

I think the disciples must have been elbowing each other, as they saw Jesus beaming with joy. Luke 10:21 says that at that very time *"He rejoiced greatly in the Holy Spirit."* What does that look like? I wonder. Did He bow his head in quiet meditation? No. Did He whirl around like David? Perhaps. Was He laughing and crying? It was joy empowered by the Holy Spirit. Here we have the original Spirit's refreshing with laughter! He exclaimed:

> I thank you, Father, Lord of heaven and earth, that You have hidden these things from the wise and prudent and revealed them to babes. Even so, Father, for so it seemed good in Your

sight . . . Blessed are the eyes which see the things you see, for I
tell you, that many prophets and kings have desired to see what
you see, and have not seen it, and to hear what you hear, and
have not heard it (Luke 10:21, 23b-24).

God was revealing something to these disciples that the prophets and kings of old
longed to see. What was it? It was the beginning of a proactive spreading of the
blessing of God. Through this activity, one day all nations would have a part of
God's Kingdom and Satan would be finally cast down from his throne of tyranny.
The Kingdom of God was spreading inch by inch, and it had just spilled over into
the Samaritans. The very thing that could tempt Jesus (Matt. 4) is also the very
point of His greatest joy!

Going After the One
We need to study what gives joy to Jesus. He is the Good Shepherd and told us
a story of a shepherd that gives us a rare glimpse into His heart. What gives joy
to our Shepherd's heart? Was it all the ninety-nine sheep that stayed at home?
No. His Shepherd heart compels Him to leave the ninety-nine and head for the
mountains to find the wayward one. Joy comes with finding the one lost sheep,
and in great excitement, He calls for His neighbors and friends to come and rejoice
with Him. (Luke 15:3-7)

What likewise brought joy to the heart of the woman? Do we see her celebrating
that at least she still has nine coins? No. She rejoices when the lost one is
discovered.

In the story of the prodigal son, what caused joy in the heart of the Father? Was it
His eldest son who stayed faithfully at home in obedience and service? No. It was
the gift of a lost son's return. A repentant, humbled, returning sinner gets heaven
all excited. The fatted calf is killed, and the party is thrown, not because the elder
son had done his duty in the fields, but because, "My son who was dead is now
alive; he was lost but now he is found!"

This joy of heaven spills over into our hearts, if we are in tune with Jesus and
His salvation agenda. Why is it that Paul in Philippians 1:4 had joy every time
he thought of and prayed for the church there? Verses 7-8 say that he felt this
way, because they were in his heart, and he longed for them with the affection of
Christ! How is it that the heart of the Savior can be found in a man? This is the
mystery: that as we pursue Christ His heart begins to reflect through our lives.

Paul was able to share in the joy of heaven regarding the Church, because he also
shared the pain, "I have great sorrow and unceasing grief in my heart . . . for the
sake of my brothers . . ." (Rom. 9:2,3). The promise is that when we weep with

those who weep, we also get to share in their joy! As we embrace the heart of Jesus in pain and discomfort, we get His joy!

I remember the first time I gave a public invitation for people to repent and find forgiveness in Christ; five young people came forward. I was thrilled. That night, I could not sleep. Tears of gratitude and excitement poured out of my eyes, pooled in my ears, and soaked my pillow. Recently, I had the same experience all over. Mostly, what God has me doing now is calling churches to obey Christ and His commission, mobilizing individuals to go to the ends of the earth, but I was privileged to lead a young man named Hector to the throne of Jesus. My spirit rejoiced with all of heaven, as this lost lamb came home.

> I tell you that there is more joy in heaven over one sinner who repents, than over the ninety-nine righteous persons who need no repentance (Luke 15:7).

Compassion of Jesus

There are two sides to this lost and found coin. The heart of Jesus was also acquainted with pain and grief. The father was lost in a sea of turmoil and despair, before his "dead" son came home. The Good Shepherd did not wait at home, sleeping in ease thinking, "If he wants to come home, he knows where our door is." Nothing so smug and careless. With great urgency, that all rescue operations deserve, He rushed out to search. In Matthew 9:37, Jesus saw the multitude and was filled with compassion, because they were like sheep that are scattered and oppressed and have no shepherd. Before the joy of recovery is claimed, we must enter into His heart of compassion.

There are some who so identify themselves with the pain of others that it is almost as though they can feel it. In some ways, I am a wimp. People tell me about paper cuts, and I have a flash back to the terrible sound and feeling and lasting sting of one that I have had. James Ferrell, a very distant cousin-in-law, likes to torture me with gross stories of terrible injuries he or others around him have endured. My stomach instantly is turning over in knots, and I feel as though I am experiencing the horrors of his story. I am not sure that it is compassion, but it is identification.

A truly compassionate person is one who suffers with you in your pain. The Sabaot tribe of Western Kenya has no word for compassion in their language. As Wycliffe Bible translators struggled to find an acceptable way of describing this crucial concept, the people coined the phrase, "God is crying with us" to mean He has compassion.[4] These are not big crocodile tears, like some TV evangelist who needs one more dollar. It is real compassion from the heart of God that always moves the hand of God.

In the Gospels, we see the most compassionate man that ever walked the earth. He is a man of intense emotion and compassion. We see Him moved to grief over the death of a friend and weeping over the city of Jerusalem.

It is not natural for us to have this deep compassion. We can hardly feel it toward those around us, let alone those on the other side of the earth. Sometimes we are so overwhelmed by the sheer amount of suffering throughout the world that we shut off our compassion. Maybe too many times of watching *Old Yeller* did our compassion in. Jesus wants to give us His heart of compassion, and the Father desires us to be conformed to the image of Christ in our actions, attitudes and emotions. We must diligently pray that He cut the calluses from our hearts, so that we might be even as He is.

S.D. Gordon wrote in His book *Quiet talks on Service*,

> There is a great word used of Jesus, and by Him, nine times in brief records, the word *compassion* . . . The word, actually used under our English, means to have the bowels or heart, the seat of emotion, greatly stirred . . . The sight of a leprous man, or of a demon-distressed man, moved Him. The great multitudes huddling together after Him, so pathetically, like leaderless sheep, eager, hungry, tired, always stirred Him to the depths. The lone woman, bleeding her heart out through her eyes, as she followed the body of her boy out — He couldn't stand that at all.[5]

Man of Sorrows
A.W. Tozer asserts,

> The Bible was written in tears and to tears it will yield its best treasures. God has nothing to say to the frivolous man. It was to Moses, a trembling man, that God spoke on the mount, and that same man later saved the nation when he threw himself before God with the offer to have himself blotted out of God's book for Israel's sake. Daniel's long season of fasting and prayer brought Gabriel from heaven to tell him the secret of the centuries. When the beloved John wept much because no one could be found worthy to open the seven-sealed book, one of the elders comforted him with the joyous news that the Lion of the tribe of Judah had prevailed.

> The psalmists often wrote in tears, the prophets could hardly conceal their heavy-heartedness, and the Apostle Paul in his otherwise joyous epistle to the Philippians broke into tears

when he thought of the many whom were enemies of the cross of Christ and whose end was destruction. Those Christian leaders who shook the world were one and all men of sorrows whose witness to mankind welled out of heavy hearts. There is no power in tears per se, but tears and power ever lie close together in the Church of the First-born.

It is not a reassuring thought that the writings of the grief-stricken prophets are often pored over by persons whose interests are curious merely and who never shed one tear for the woes of the world."[6]

We need not fear the emotional heart of God. It is a blessing to enter into the depth of His friendship. I was once so overwhelmed by the images He was sharing with me that I felt my spirit would be forever crushed. I could only pray in sobs as He showed me the nations and peoples of the world that are still scattered sheep, oppressed and have no Shepherd. I asked Him, "What can I do?" and He seemed to say, *"It isn't so much that I wanted you to come up with a solution, I just wanted a friend to cry with."*

Notes

1. G. Christian Weiss, *God's Plan Man's Need Our Mission* (Lincoln: Back to the Bible Publication, 1971), p. 137.
2. Moyer, Larry, Dallas Theological Seminary's "Kindred Spirits: Regaining a Heart for Unbelievers" Vol. 18, No. 3, Autumn, 1994.
3. Rev. Elon Foster, *New Encyclopedia of Prose Illustrations* (New York: T.Y. Crowell, 1877), p. 180.
4. Wycliffe Bible Translators, "The Word Like a River" (1995).
5. S. D. Gordon, *Quiet Talks On Service* (New York: Fleming H. Revell Company, 1906), pp. 87, 88.
6. A. W. Tozer, *God Tells the Man Who Cares* (Camp Hill, PA: Christian Publications, 1992), pp. 2-3.

fourteen

Who Do You Say I Am?

"**His heart** goes out to the masses."[1]
Keith Green

"It gratifies **His heart** and it glorifies His name to pardon,
justify and accept a penitent soul that
simply believes in Jesus."
C. H. Mackintosh

Angels Behind Every Bush

Christmas is that time of the year when the world seems full of angels . . . I mean the paper type in windows, or especially of late, the little figurines of overweight (chubabims), little smiling guys that look more like Cupid than Michael.

This year angels are really vogue. I can hardly wash my hands without wrestling with the theological implications of using soap that looks like an angel. Christmas marketers are deftly using the holy ones for profit. Our televisions are barraged, and every billboard endures a season-long assault of flying messengers advertising some sale at the mall.

They have one thing right. Angels are messengers. The word we translate angel is *evangelist*. Christmas seems to bring them out in droves . . . it always has . . . you remember the first Christmas? On that first Christmas, I think the angels could not contain it any longer. Here He was — their King and the Salvation that humans so needed and the nations desired — being born, in the most humble, human situation, no fanfare allowed, not even an advance room reservation. These angels, I think, were bursting, and God said, "OK . . . let loose on those few shepherds." What an announcement! I bring you good tidings (news) of great joy which will be for **all people**. For there is born to you this day in the city of David a savior, who is Christ the Lord . . . Glory to God in the highest and **on earth peace among men** with whom God is well pleased (Luke 2:10b, 11, 14).

111

Who Do You Say That I Am?

> Angels sent by God
> Proclaiming the birth of Salvation
> To people who didn't know Him
> Telling them that He may be found.

These angels seemed so eager and capable. Everyone they told believed and did as they were instructed. It seems a bit peculiar that Jesus would then commission us to be His angels. We are to be His messengers of the Good News of Great Joy. Now, I know you are no angel . . . but so long as there are whole peoples who have never heard about Jesus, He has commanded us to go to them. There are still millions who have never heard that Jesus was born. They still sit in darkness and have never seen the Great Light dawning on them. (Isaiah 9) It is this Great News that has yet to be announced.

Yet, like practicing angels, we sing to each other in choirs in beautifully decorated churches while the unreached wait to be told this news for the first time. All Christmas season long, we try to outdo our neighbor's church by putting on the most elaborate productions known to man, complete with fully functional camels, along with their pooper-scoopers. We even have the technology to dangle live "angels" from the rafters. Our free time is spent caroling outside each other's homes with evangelistic fervor. It is little more than practice, our singing about this "old, old story."

It is meant to be new! Something new and good for those who have never heard. It is to be Good News for an earth that has yet to receive her King. The true Christmas Spirit is not so wrapped up in how we celebrate, but how we announce. It has less to do with our church party, than the missionary task. Christmas has more to do with where the Good News has not yet been, than where it already exists.

You and I are commissioned to be angels and go to the ends of the earth. Jesus, through us and our human frailties, becomes that Great Light that the unreached will see. It is our testimony to those who have never heard that is the Good News of Great Joy that is for all peoples. For there is born the Savior, who is Jesus Christ the Lord, "Emmanuel." He has come as a man, humbling Himself to live as one of us.

Those who lay down their Christmas pageants and become angels to the unreached, their lives will become a song saying, "Glory to God in the highest, and to those on earth, peace to all who through Christ have been made pleasing to God."

> We are sent by God
> To proclaim Christ, their Salvation
> To peoples who did not know Him
> Telling them that He may be found.

The Man Who Could Not Die

The angels were not the only ones who recognized the global Good News that Jesus was. You remember the prophet Simeon. He was the guy who had made a deal with God that he would not die before he saw the Messiah. He knew the purpose of the Messiah, and as he held Baby Jesus in his arms, he prayed this prayer:

> . . . he took Him in his arms and blessed God and said, "Lord, now You are letting Your servant depart in peace, according to Your word; For my eyes have seen Your salvation which **You have prepared before the face of all peoples, a light to bring revelation to the Gentiles** *(nations)*, and the glory of Your people Israel" (Luke 2:28-32).

Though he was a prophet in Israel's temple, he understood that Jesus was so much more than just for Israel. He was to be a Light to the Nations. Simeon understood. He had that revelation.

The Friend of the Bridegroom

Even John the Baptist knew the global implications of Jesus. He was to prepare the way for the Messiah. For what purpose? So that all mankind might see the Savior.

> . . . As it is written in the book of Isaiah the prophet, saying: "The voice of one crying in the wilderness: "Prepare the way of the Lord; make His paths straight. Every valley shall be filled and every mountain and hill brought low; The crooked places shall be made straight and the rough ways smooth; **and all flesh shall see the salvation of God"** (Luke 3:4-6).

His job description is ours as well. Those who have been called into ministry are also called to prepare the Bride for the Bridegroom, to be His friend. John's job and ours is to remove the obstacles that are keeping the peoples of the world from seeing Christ. Whatever it is that is keeping them from the Gospel (shy of repentance and the cross) needs to be conquered. Language must be overcome; culture must be adapted to; distances must be traversed; comforts removed; prejudice repented of; spiritual blinders removed, that He might be seen in all his glory, and the nations have a chance at His great salvation!

When John finally saw Jesus working His way through the crowds to be baptized, He cried out, "Behold the Lamb of God who takes away the sins of the world!" John knew several things about Jesus that many others did not seem to know of the Messiah. Jesus was sent for death. Why must He die? For the sins of the world! With jubilation we proclaim the Lamb who is worthy, was slain, and with

His blood has purchased men from among every tongue, tribe and nation! John was singing this song before any of his contemporaries, but he was not the first. Those who were intimate with the heart of God, His dreams and ambitions, plans and purposes, knew that the Messiah was for all nations.

The description of John the Baptist, *"The voice of one crying in the wilderness,"* is from Isaiah. Isaiah knew about Jesus and His purposes. How did these guys, hundreds of years before Jesus appeared, know about Him, His suffering and His purposes, when it seemed like the disciples who were Jesus' friends were quite clueless? The secret is their intimacy with God and an understanding of His heart. David could prophesy about the Messiah, because he was a man after God's heart. Jeremiah could prophesy about the Messiah, because He was a man that embraced the emotional heart of God. He was known as the prophet of tears, full of God's compassion. Isaiah also was part of this rare group who was a friend of God, who had his ear to God's breast, hearing the beat of His heart. God's secrets became theirs.

While listening to God, Isaiah overheard a conversation in Heaven about the purpose of the Suffering Servant, the Messiah, which is Jesus Christ. Many supposed that the Messiah was for the political salvation of Israel. But Isaiah heard from God the global purpose of Jesus Christ:

> Indeed He says, "It is too small a thing that You should be My Servant to raise up the tribes of Jacob and to restore the preserved ones of Israel; I will also give You as a **light to the nations**, that You should be My **salvation to the ends of the earth**" (Is. 49:6).

God said, *"It is too small of a thing for you just to rescue Israel. That is not your only purpose. I am going to send you as salvation to the ends of the earth."*

Messiah and God

How much did Jesus understand His purpose for the nations? The encounter with Nathaniel is very revealing. (John 1:45-51) Philip had met Jesus and was thoroughly convinced that Jesus was indeed the One that Moses and the prophets had written about. However, when Philip told Nathaniel about Jesus, that He was from Nazareth and the son of Joseph, Nathaniel's snide remark was, "Can anything good come out of Nazareth?" I guess Nathaniel, against his own "better" judgment, decided to go and check out this Jesus. As Jesus saw him approaching, He said, "Behold, an Israelite indeed, in whom is no guile!" Nathaniel was surprised, "How do You know me?" Jesus answered and said to him, "Before Philip called you, when you were under the fig tree, I saw you."

We often think of Thomas the Doubter's confession, "My Lord, my God," when he saw Jesus with the wounds in His hands, as one of the greatest confessions of the New Testament. Or we think of Peter, when he said, "You are the Messiah" but here, the Holy Spirit fell on Nathaniel and he uttered one of the greatest confessions of all time: Nathaniel answered and said to Him, "Rabbi, You are the Son of God! You are the King of Israel!" Nathaniel recognized right away that standing before Him was Deity, the Son of God. Not only that, but Jesus was the awaited King of Israel. Jesus was the Messiah.

Though Nathaniel's confession was quite possibly one of the greatest, his understanding was not complete, and Jesus was not content to leave it in this realm of good, but quickly classified it as "not good enough." Jesus said to him, "Most assuredly, I say to you, hereafter you shall see heaven open, and the angels of God ascending and descending upon the Son of Man" (John 1:49-51). Jesus refused to accept the title Son of God which was Deity and the King of Israel which was Messiahship over Israel. Instead, He chose for Himself a greater title: The Son of Man. Why is this a greater title?

Look at Daniel 7:13-14:

> I was watching in the night visions, and behold, One like the Son of Man, coming with the clouds of heaven! He came to the Ancient of Days, and they brought Him near before Him. Then to Him was given dominion and glory and a kingdom, that all peoples, nations, and languages should serve Him. His dominion is an everlasting dominion, which shall not pass away, and His kingdom the one which shall not be destroyed.

It was not good enough that Nathaniel recognized Him as God, which many people do. Nor was it good enough that He was recognized as Messiah, the Promised One. Jesus desired to be known as the Son of Man. This title defined His ministry. It reflected His desire for the peoples of the world and the global nature of His ministry.

Some may say that He did not really understand what He was doing here, by calling Himself the Son of Man. Lots of people could be called the Son of Man, they argue. No. He understood what He was saying. Later, Jesus talks again about Himself:

> When the Son of Man comes in His glory, and all the holy angels with Him, then He will sit on the throne of His glory. All the nations will be gathered before Him, and He will separate them one from another, as a shepherd divides his sheep from the goats (Matt. 25:31, 32).

Who Do You Say That I Am?

Jesus knew exactly what He was saying. He is the King of all the world. He is the God of all peoples, nations, tongues, and tribes. He is satisfied with nothing less than total global dominion.

Notes

1. Keith Green, "Keith Green Memorial Concert," (Tyler, TX: Last Days Ministries, 1982).
2. C.H. Mackintosh, *The Great Commission, Miscellaneous Writings, Volume IV* (New York: Loizeaux Brothers, 1898) p. GC-19.

fifteen

Teaching Them...
Everything

"To understand our mission to witness and our mission to
welcome our fellow men to the love of Christ, we must
start with the source of missions. They do not begin with
men: their origin is found in the **heart of God**. When we
know what he intends to do, we can believe and
work for the accomplishment of his will,
the coming of his kingdom."[1]
David Brainerd Woodward

The Full Gospel

"Are you a Full Gospel Christian? Is your church a Full Gospel Church?" Fred
Markert, founder of Strategic Frontiers YWAM in Colorado Springs, was asking
the whole church. They responded in stunned silence, of course they were full
Gospel, who goes to a church that says, "We are a half Gospel church"? What is
a half Gospel church anyway? One that tithes only 5%, or you only have to come
every other Sunday? Sermons are only 15 minutes, and only the first half of the
commandments are binding?

Fred asked for the congregation in one sentence to summarize the Gospel. Most
yelled something like: "Freedom from the penalty of sin!" "Eternal life!" After
many of those true answers came forth, Fred, with his great smile, pointed out
Galatians 3:8, and the glaring
omission in their gospel:

> And the Scripture, foreseeing that God would justify the
> Gentiles by faith, preached the gospel to Abraham beforehand,
> saying, "In you all the nations shall be blessed" (Gal. 3:8).

Teaching Them... Everything

Have you ever thought about missions as an integral part of the Gospel? We mostly consider missions what we do with the Good News, but this command to take the Gospel to all nations is actually part of the Good News — that all nations will have a part in this. You are not fully discipled in the Gospel, nor have you fully received the Good News, unless you have been taught to obey and are actively embracing the commandment, "Go and make disciples of all nations." It is part of the Gospel.

There is much about the Gospel that we seem not to understand. When my daughter Jessica was just learning how to write. She was doing pretty well at sounding out words and then writing them down. One day she came in with a piece of paper with her name spelled Jessica Zuwit. It was close. She assumed she knew how our last named sounded, and so wrote it down like she thought it should be.

The Gospel and the Great Commission can be that way. I started out understanding the Great Commission as meaning that I should make friends with the kids that were not so popular in school. By college, the Great Commission meant compassionate ministries in the inner cities of America, so I worked in San Francisco at Height-Ashbury for a season. Like a child learning how to spell her name, I understood more and more clearly the breadth and depth of the Great Commission and the teachings of Jesus. May we learn to submit ourselves to the teaching of the Holy Spirit, who can teach us and lead us into all truth.

Jesus' Teachings

Even Jesus' everyday, common teaching displayed God's heart for the nations. In Luke 10, Jesus tells us the Greatest Commandment and its second, inextricable part:

> So He answered and said, "You shall love the Lord your God with all your heart, with all your soul, with all your strength, and with all your mind," and "your neighbor as yourself" (Luke 10:27).

Love Him with everything — full abandon. Do not hold back anything for yourself. By the way, this is the essence of right relationship. *"I will bless you. I will be in right relationship with you. This is your part. Love Me with your whole heart, soul, strength and mind. Be in right relationship with Me."* We must be people who pursue God with our whole heart, not hold a bit back for ourselves; love Him until there is room for nothing else. Enough of these false teachers who try and tell us to take our God in doses, "Now don't get extreme on us." This is the voice of compromise, Jesus says love God with everything we have, and then He proceeded to illustrate His intended meaning.

This Great Commandment is a repeat of the Genesis 12 Covenant formula: I will bless you, and you will be a blessing to the nations. I know. I made a jump from neighbor to nation, and some of you may be scratching your head. Remember the story of the little old lady, who came out of Church shaking the pastor's hand while saying, "I just love your sermons so! You get so much out of the Bible that isn't even there..." I do not want to be pulling one of those. Keep reading in Luke Chapter 10 and you will see what I mean.

The second part of this commandment is: "Love your neighbor as yourself." Jesus goes on. You remember the lawyer. He was not happy with that. The lawyer asked, "Who exactly is my neighbor?" He did not really want to lavish love on everyone around him, and so he wanted to know "exactly who is my neighbor." Is there a loophole to justify some sort of lack of love for Tony down the street? Jesus saw his heart, and He sees ours also. We do not want to be responsible for much beyond our borders of convenience, comfort and distance, so He told a story. He gave an example of that love, and what He gave was a cross-cultural love — a Good Samaritan to Jew.

Do you see what Jesus is saying? Right relationship with God and extension of that right relationship to every tongue, tribe and nation on planet earth are interconnected. He gives the same pattern through the Great Commandment that He gave in the Great Covenant — that Genesis 12 pattern: "I will bless you and through you all nations will be blessed."

Lord's Prayer

> In this manner, therefore, pray: "Our Father in heaven, hallowed be Your name. Your kingdom come. Your will be done on earth as it is in heaven" (Matt. 6:9-10).

Before we pray for our daily bread, which our bodies need for survival, and before we pray for spiritual protection from the enemy of our souls, we are to pray that His Name is honored in all the earth and that His will is done among the peoples of this planet, even as it is by the inhabitants of heaven.

How strange that our personal needs — our need for sin to be forgiven, or our need for an amount of money or our need for protection against the enemy — always comes first in our prayers, to the point that we rarely get to the topics that we are commanded to pray first. Jesus knew our weaknesses, and so He ordered the prayer this way on purpose to guarantee that His global mission would get prayer and concern.

Jesus was, of course, assuming that we are students wanting to learn how to pray and then, that we actually do get around to prayer. I have been to many prayer meetings that are mostly talk, or if prayer is involved, it is usually about some sick person who is not even present in our meeting. If you call some mission agencies' prayer hot lines, the prayer requests that you will hear are often not about dark territories that need Jesus and about the bold proclamation of the Gospel. Instead, they are long lists of missionaries (current and retired) and their ailments. Prayer is not primarily our drive-through intercom at a fast food restaurant, where we order our long list of desires. We are commanded to *"Seek first His kingdom and all these other things will be added unto you."* But we seek to add these other things to us, and then once in a while, we fire up an unemotional appeal for His Kingdom's establishment over there somewhere . . . Africa maybe.

We are to pray that God's will be done on earth, as it is in heaven. Do you want to know what God's will is for that man walking by on the street? "God is not willing that any should perish, but that all should come to repentance" (2 Pet. 3:9). Do you want to pray in accordance with God's will? Let us put aside theology for a moment. Just pray scripture. I know what God's will is for that man — that he be saved.

When you are watching the news and some event is taking place in Bangladesh, and you are thinking, "Oh, that's terrible." When a tornado goes through Bangladesh, it picks up those tin roofs that they have weighted down with little rocks, and it starts swirling them like giant machetes, and they slash through the homes killing hundreds — simple tornadoes. We hardly ever hear about it, but when you do see it on the news, you can know how to pray. Pray God's will. They are in a dark country without access to the Gospel. How are you going to pray? Pray that God in His mercy makes His salvation known to them, that they turn and repent. Pray that God's will be done on earth, as it is in heaven. You are praying scripture, not an imagination of man.

1 John 5:19 says, "The whole world lies under the sway of the wicked one." So when we pray, as we are told to in the Lord's prayer, "Thy Kingdom come," we are actually offensively engaging in an attack on the kingdom of the enemy, the prince of this world. We are praying that God and His Kingdom take over. In this spiritual warfare, any Christian who does not participate is guilty of treason.

Kingdom of Heaven
Matthew 13 is all about the Kingdom of Heaven. The Kingdom of Heaven is like this. The Kingdom of Heaven is like that. Make sure you have your Bible out to look at this passage together with me. Let us start with verse 31:

> Another parable He put forth to them, saying: "The kingdom of heaven is like a mustard seed, which a man took and sowed in his field, which indeed is the least of all the seeds; but when it is grown it is greater than the garden plants and becomes a

tree, so that the birds of the air come and nest in its branches"
(Matt. 13:31-32).

The implication is that it becomes the largest tree and all the birds of the air can find roost in its branches. Here it is. This will give you great understanding. Jesus is trying to give us a glimpse into the Kingdom of Heaven here, and He is using these illustrations to explain it. It is something that starts small, but it is going to keep growing until all the birds of the air can find a home in it. Maybe that does not bless you yet. To really bless you, you need to read the next parable, which is immediately after it.

> Another parable He spoke to them: "The kingdom of heaven is like leaven, which a woman took and hid in three measures of meal till it was all leavened" (Matt. 13:33).

Stay with me here. I know that some of you are starting to roll your eyes and wander. Read it again . . .The Kingdom of Heaven is like some yeast put in some dough. This lady comes along and starts to mix the dough. She is making bread. She takes a little bit of yeast and stirs the yeast into the dough. She stirs and kneads until the entire dough has yeast spread throughout it. As long as there is a clump of dough somewhere that has no yeast, she is going to mush it around. She is going to keep working it, because she wants the whole dough evenly yeasted. That is when it is done.

This is what God has always been about: getting the Kingdom of God to permeate the world — the glory of the knowledge of the Lord covering the earth as the waters cover the sea. The process is not complete until the whole amount is leavened with this Good News. He will continue to knead the dough, forcing Christians out among the unreached nations, or as we see in the USA, clumps of unreached "dough" (immigrants) being forced in upon our once "Christian" neighborhoods. God is not the God of ethnic purity but of Kingdom expansion! He loves to mix it up!

This is a little glimpse into God's desire for His people. We are the yeast that He takes and pushes into the world, and He keeps moving us. He keeps doing it until we fill the earth. We are to be fruitful and multiply and fill the earth. The Kingdom is going to keep growing. You are going to see the Church continue to expand and branch out, reaching into new areas, becoming larger. By the way, the Church is the largest thing in the garden right now. Evangelical Christianity is growing twice as fast as the nearest religion.[2] The branches of the Kingdom of Heaven are going to keep growing until all the birds of the air — all the peoples of the earth — can find a home in it.

Teaching Them... Everything

Chocolate Chip Cookie Surprise

It is kind of a funny statement. Does anybody still make homemade chocolate chip cookies? I know you can buy them in loaf style in the store and cut them off. The only thing those are good for is sticking a spoon in them and keeping them in the refrigerator. I still prefer the homemade chocolate chip cookies myself. Guys, this may shock you, but there is salt in them! If you have a chocolate chip cookie without salt, it is not a very good thing. It is not very tasty — kind of bland. Have you ever had chocolate chip cookie surprise? That is when the cook adds the salt but does not mix it very well, so you bite into the cookie and get a mouth full of salt. It is not very pleasant. Salt is meant to be in there, but it is not meant to be clumped. Salt is meant to be sprinkled, not poured into your food. That is why we have shakers. A shaker spreads it evenly throughout the whole dish. Matthew 5:13-14 says, "You are the world's salt." We are the world's salt and not meant to be clumped. We are to be spread out evenly throughout the earth.

Farmer Jesus

"The Kingdom of Heaven may be compared to a man who sowed good seed in his field" (Matt. 13:28). This passage goes on to tell more about the bad guys that came along and sowed tares in among the wheat. Later on, the disciples were quite confused and in Verse 36, they came to Jesus and said, "Explain to us the parable of the tares of the field." And Jesus answered . . .

> "He who sows the good seed is the Son of Man. The field is
> the world, the good seeds are the sons of the kingdom . . ."
> (Matt. 13:37-38a).

The man who sows the seed — the farmer, who is he? Jesus. The Son of Man. He is the farmer. Where is the field? **The world.** The whole thing, not just one small portion. Who are the seeds? We are.

I know a little bit about farming. Let us say I am sowing wheat. I buy a bag of good seed. I do not want just any sort of seed. I want quality seed, because I want a high yield. Then I go to a corner of my field — any corner. I carefully rip the bag open (because later I am going to use the bag for clothing), and then I tip the bag over and pour it out, making sure I get all the seed out of the bag. I shake it out really well, because I do not want to waste any seed. There, I have a big pile of seed there in the corner of my field. I fold up the bag and take it back to Jamie who is going to sew me something nice. Man, I tell you, farming is tough work.

Did I do anything wrong? (Yeah, I know how to milk them pigs and slop them cows real good.) That's me, farmer John. Yes, well, I missed a big part, didn't I? It is called *sowing* the seed. The purpose of sowing the seed is to spread it evenly. Where? In the whole field, not just piled in one corner. Not just sowing one row or two rows. The purpose is to sow the seed all across the field evenly.

Okay. Who is the farmer again? Jesus is the farmer. Who is the seed? We are! And where are we to be sown? In the whole world! Dear friends, if we are indeed the seed of the Living God, the Farmer, and the field is His world, do not be surprised if He wants to sow you in some areas that have not been sown before. The Father loves the peoples of planet earth, and He continues to sow us to the ends of the earth. James Gilmour, the great pioneer to the nomads of Mongolia, spoke in similar fashion when he convictingly said:

> To me the question was not "Why go?" but "Why not go?" Even on the low ground of common sense I seemed called to be a missionary. For is the kingdom not a harvest field? Then I thought it only reasonable to seek the work where the work was most abundant and the workers were fewest.[3]

My friend, Nate Wilson, while working for Caleb Project helping to mobilize the Church to finish the Great Commission and, in His free time, studying for His Master's degree, shared this tidbit with me:

> The passage states, "The harvest is plentiful, but the laborers are few. Pray therefore the Lord of the harvest to send forth laborers into His harvest field." (Matt. 9:37-38) Two words stand out in the Greek text: The main verb is not the usual word for "pray" it is an intense word meaning to "beg out of a deep sense of need." Likewise, the word for "send forth" is a very forceful word meaning to "throw out" or "evict." There must be a sense of **urgency** in our prayers for God to raise up missionaries, and we must also be willing to be **wrenched out** of our own comfort zones to become missionaries ourselves![4]

Henry Martyn, the pioneer missionary to India and Persia, gave his life in serving Jesus and translating the Bible. Though He was barely thirty-one years old when he died in 1812, he had tapped into something of Jesus that few other Europeans in that age or this have recognized: "The Spirit of Christ is the Spirit of missions, and the nearer we get to Him the more intensely missionary we must become."[5] As we draw close to Christ and understand Him through His teachings, **His missionary heart** is unavoidable. If we are to follow Him and be people who are called by His Name, then we too must reflect His missionary ambition and love.

Notes
1. David Brainerd Woodward, *God, Men and Missions,* (Gospel Light Publications, 1964), p. 7.
2. Patrick Johnstone, *The Church is Bigger than You Think* (Pasadena, CA: William Carey Library Publishers, 1998), p. 111.
3. Robert Hall Glover, *The Bible Basis of Missions* (Los Angeles: Bible House of Los Angeles, 1946), p. 139.
4. Nate Wilson, Excerpted from his newsletter (with permission).
5. Frank Mead, *The Encyclopedia of Religious Quotations* (London: Peter Davies, Ltd., 1965), p. 308.

sixteen

No Go, No Lo

"If God calls you to be a missionary,
don't stoop to be a king."[1]
Jordan Grooms

"For the eyes of the Lord move to and fro throughout the
earth that He may strongly support those whose heart is
completely His."
2 Chron. 16:9

My Sunday School teacher taught me this verse: *"For God so loved the world that He gave His one and only Son that whoever believes in Him shall not perish but have eternal life" (John 3:16).* She went on to instruct me on how to apply this verse to myself by taking *the world* out and substituting my name in its place: "For God so loved *John* that He gave His one and only Son that if *John* believes in Him he shall not perish but have eternal life." Yes, that is exactly where I should find myself, if I am in the world. Is that not right? If I am lost, apart from Christ, and I am in the world, I need to know that God's love is for me, that He died for me. That is where I am in the picture — if I am in the world.

However, once we are redeemed by the blood of the Lamb, our position in this verse and our role in God's plan changes. We are in Christ, as Paul said. Being believers, we are "sons of God," Jesus being the "first born among many brothers." We need to find our lives in a new place. It is not: "For God so loved *John*" now. It is: "For God so loved *the world.*" Put *the world* back in — the whole world, every part of it. "That He gave His one and only Son, Jesus Christ, and continues to give His *sons and daughters* — those who are in Christ — that whoever believes in Jesus *through us* shall not perish but have eternal life." Do you see how our picture changes when we are in Christ and no longer in the world?

Our imagination tells us that God values us more than God values others. However, the Shepherd who left the ninety-nine to go after the lost one is most certainly more

127

concerned with those who are under the heavy yoke of Islam or are slaughtered under the hand of demonic Hinduism than about us and our comfortable, Gospel lighted homes. Jesus *"is the propitiation for our sins; and not ours only, but also the sins of the whole world"* (1 John 2:2).

It seems that new Bibles with commentaries are coming out all the time. You can buy *The Men's Devotional Bible. The Women's Devotional Bible.* You have then *The Holy Spirit Bible*, *The Wesleyan Bible*, *The Disciples' Bible*, *The Some of the Gifts of the Holy Spirit Minus Tongues Bible.* You have all different kinds of Bibles out there. We have all seen them. They are basically commentaries on one of the major versions: NASB, NIV, Living, KJV and NKJV. I always go to some of my favorite passages and see what they have to say. For example:

> All power in heaven and earth has been given to Me. Therefore, Go and make disciples of every ethne, baptizing them in the name of the Father, the Son and the Holy Spirit, teaching them to obey everything I've commanded you, and lo I am with you always, even to the end of the age (Matt. 28:19-20).

Ralph Winter, missionary and founder of the U.S. Center for World Mission, tells the story of looking at one edition (It will remain anonymous. Check your Bible.), and it said about the above verse, "Whenever you are down or lonely, or old and the house is empty, remember that Jesus is always with you. He will never leave you." Well, yes. There is nothing theologically incorrect about that, but is that what this verse is really saying? Though he claims it is not original with him, Ralph Winter, concluded, "We can reduce this verse down to: No go, no lo."[2] You see, the promise of "lo He is with you always even to the end of the age" is contingent upon your obedience to the "Go and make disciples of all nations." They are partners with each other. Sometimes we take the Bible and make it our warm fuzzy Promise Book and ignore all the commands. Can you see how the commentator mentioned above was using scripture to feel good? It is dangerous when we only focus on the parts of scripture that give us a boost. When we do this, we miss God's passion for the nations. Many of you have been looking at scripture this way. It is human nature. We love to know God's blessing for us, and it is hard for us to obey the *"Go."*

Out of Whack

A false balance is an abomination to the Lord (Prov. 11:1).

In the Church today, we sometimes place an inaccurate value on issues. We devalue what should be more important, and we give more emphasis to that which is of less value. In the name of "balance," we often relegate the Great Commission to last place. Pastors seem to tip the scales toward personal issues and ignore the greater issues, very similar to the Pharisees who tithed their mint and their dill, but they ignored the greater issues of justice and mercy (Matt. 23:23): ***Justice*** — that all fall short of God's glory and some day will be judged and the ***mercy*** — that God so loved the world that He gave His only Son that He is not willing that any should perish, but that all should come to repentance. The weightier issues of justice and mercy, as found in the Great Commission, are often relegated to insignificance, and insignificants are given prominence. "A false balance is an abomination to the Lord" (Prov. 11:1).

I know of whole ministries that are self-proclaimed, heresy hunters. They write books and have radio shows that major on attacking perceived enemies of Christ. It seems that their heresies all focus on issues of creed and methodology, while ignoring the greater anti-christs in Christendom. Yes, it is heresy to deny Christ's words, "I and the Father are one." But is it not of equal heresy to ignore Jesus' command to "Go and make disciples of all nations?" One can be an orthodox Church in every way: great structure, good theology, excellent sermons and teaching, lots of giving; but if the Great Commission is not taught and obeyed, it is a heretical church.

> And Jesus came and spoke to them saying, "All authority has been given to me in heaven and on earth. Go therefore and make disciples of all the nations *(panta ta ethne - all the ethnics: tongues tribes and peoples)*, baptizing them in the name of the Father, Son and the Holy Spirit, teaching them to observe all things that I have commanded you; and lo, I am with you always, even to the end of the age" (Matt. 28:18-20).

Why do we call this the "Great" Commission? First, it is a great claim. Jesus claims to have all authority in heaven and earth. Then, there is a great command to go and make disciples of all nations, and finally, there is a great promise that He will always be with us. Even though He gave us this giant task of making disciples of all the peoples of planet earth, we are not to focus on the size of the job, but rather we are to focus on the size of our great God. He has all authority and power. He is the one who is going to be with us. We are to be potential oriented rather than problem oriented. Adoniram Judson said, "The future is as bright as the promises of God."[3] William Carey preached, "Expect great things from God. Attempt great things for God."[4]

His Commission

> So Jesus said to them again, "Peace to you! As the Father has sent me, I also send you" (John 20:21).

No Go, No Lo

Jesus said, *"Do the same task in the same way that I did." "In the same way the Father sent me, I am sending you."* Suddenly, verses like John 3:16 are no longer catechism verses. They are marching orders. "For God so loved the world that He gave His one and only Son, that whoever believes in Him shall not perish but have eternal life." "As the Father sent me, so send I you." "I did not come to be served, but to serve and to give my life as a ransom for many." "As the Father sent me, so send I you." Do you see it? They are no longer little verses we memorize about Jesus. They are verses about us, our calling and our commission. As He came to lay down His life, so He is calling us to lay down our lives for the peoples of the world.

In clear, easy to understand language, Jesus states that He came to "seek and save that which was lost." (Luke 19:10) In one of His parables, He clearly calls rebellious mankind the sheep that have gone astray. He, being the Good Shepherd, finds them and brings them safely back. And though there are the lost sheep of Israel that He is concerned about, He also tells of sheep which are not of this fold that He must bring in. (John 10:11-18) He is the Good Shepherd that lays down His life for the sheep. Why did the Father send Him? To seek and save that which is lost.

When Jesus gave us the commission of "as the father sent me so send I you," He was also commissioning us to go and find the lost sheep from among every tongue, tribe, and nation. There are still multitudes that are like sheep without a shepherd, and God calls us to bring them into His fold.

> My flock wandered through all the mountains and on every high
> hill, and my flock was scattered over all the surface of the earth;
> And there was no one to search or seek for them (Ez. 34:6).

What about the millions of unreached people scattered over the surface of the world that have never yet heard the mention of His Name? Who will care for all those who are so far from His fold and have never heard the call of the Shepherd? Is it not clearly our mission to go seek these people? God sent Him into the world that the world might be saved (John 3:17); even so God sends us into the world, that they might be saved.

> But you shall receive power when the Holy Spirit has come
> upon you; and you shall be witnesses to Me in Jerusalem, and in
> all Judea and Samaria, and to the end of the earth (Acts 1:8).

These are the last words of Christ — the most important. Here He introduces us to the scope of the disciples' ministry. The disciples were not supposed to finish it in Jerusalem, then go on to Judea, then Samaria, and only then to the ends of the earth. It was and, and, and, and. "You're going to be ministering to

130

all these places at once." By the way, Jerusalem was not their hometown. Many people have used this verse to support the view that we are to witness first in our hometown. The only problem with that line of logic is that these disciples were not from Jerusalem; they were Galileans! It was like Oklahomans in New York City. They stuck out like a sore thumb. Remember Peter's denial of Christ? "Surely you're a Galilean," the servant girl said, "You must be one of them. I mean, you've got the same accent." Peter's gutless reply: "Curse, curse, curse, I am not." You remember that whole scene. These disciples stuck out. They were Galileans (that land of Gentiles up north). God told them to go to Jerusalem for a specific strategic reason and from there launch a worldwide ministry. We should never assume that just because we are from an area, that this is where God wants us, we must listen to him. If He tells an Okie to go minister in New York City or Urumqi, China, then *Go!*

Copy Cats

Though some of the Gospels contain things that others do not, they basically tell the same story of Jesus' life. You would think that the miraculous birth would be in each of them, but the nativity is only in two of the Gospels. Yet Christmas, the big party, is probably the focus of our entire year. Financially, for churches and churchgoers alike, it is a significant expense. There is only one miracle that is repeated in all four of the Gospels — the Feeding of the Five Thousand. (I think that we celebrate this event at Thanksgiving, when we all get up from the table feeling like we ate enough for five thousand.) Importantly, the Great Commission is in five: Matthew, Mark, Luke, John and Acts.

Even more intriguing is that all of the Great Commissions do not seem to be reports of the same scene. It is not as though they were all at the same seminar saying, "Oh, that's good. I've got to remember that one. Write it down. Mark, do you mind if I compare notes later on this one? Okay, so go into all the nations. I get the idea". They were not all reporting from the same event. All of the commissions have different circumstances and audiences. Some are in the north, in Galilee. Some are in Jerusalem. They are all over the map. Neither were the different commissions said to the same crowd. Once, Jesus appeared to several hundred and said it. Another time He appeared to two and said it. Once it was to a room full of people. It was said to different groups.

I think there is probably a very plausible explanation. Perhaps the post-resurrection mind was not as good as we thought it was. *"Okay, go and make disciples of all nations." "Stop me if I've said this before. I want you to go and make disciples of all nations."* Do you think that was the problem? Do you think maybe He was not up to par? No. He knew it was important. Jesus, in essence, said, *"I've got limited time. I'm only here on earth for forty more days. I'm going to underline and underline something very important that I want no one to miss. I don't care if you miss a lot, but don't miss this: that repentance and forgiveness of sins is to be preached among all the nations."* He said it over and over again, yet how easily it has become a marginal issue in our Christianity. It is for a special interest group. It is competition with our Children's Ministry for dollars. The very thing that God left us on earth to do and that He commanded us to finish, we treat as the Great Suggestion. We hardly even know it is there. "Go and make disciples of all nations" was the commandment of Jesus five times over.

Whose Fault?

This is the last message of Keith Green, one of this century's great prophets and musicians. Shortly after this message was delivered in 1982, Keith was killed in a plane crash.

> My wife and I just returned from a trip overseas visiting missionary bases, and it opened our eyes to a couple of facts. One of them was that God is not an American. But the world belongs to Him, and He loves everybody the same. He loves you and every other person whether they're known or forgotten, and His heart goes out to the masses. It says in the Bible, "It is not God's will that anyone should perish, but that all should come to repentance."

> But as I traveled around, and I saw whole nations of people where there were only 50 or 100 believers in the whole country, what I saw was it's either God's will for it to be this way, or it's got to be somebody else's fault. It's not God's fault that the world isn't being won . . . no, there is no fault in God. And I already told you what His Bible says: "It's not His will for anyone to perish."

> There is a command in the Bible that says, "Go ye into all the nations and preach the Gospel unto every creature and make disciples of men." We like to think, well, that was for the disciples. You know, that was for the apostles. That's for the missionaries. That's for humanitarians. That's for real Christians. I mean, really, they're so spiritual they can't stay in society, so they've got to go overseas and bury themselves in some tribe somewhere down in the Amazon. But I'll tell you what, folks, the world isn't being won today, because we're not doing it. It's our fault. This generation of Christians is responsible for this generation of souls on the earth, and nowhere in the world is the Gospel so plentiful as in the United States! Nowhere. I don't want to see us stand before God on that day and say, "But God, I didn't hear you call me." Here's something for you to chew on. You didn't need to hear a call — you're already called! In fact,

if you stay home from going into all nations, you had better be able to say to God, "You called me to stay home, God. I know that as a fact." Unless God tells you otherwise, you are called!

Now don't go out and sell everything you own and leave tomorrow. Get some training. You don't need a college degree, necessarily. It sure is a good reason to go to college, though. I know so many kids that go to college that don't even know that God has told them to go and don't even know why they're there! Everybody else in church is going, and Mom and Dad want them to go. That's good enough for them. But I'll tell you what. It isn't good enough for Jesus. He wants you to be in His army, and He wants you to take orders from Him. And sure, He wants you to submit to your parents, but He wants you to find out what your Father in Heaven says first. What does He have to say to you? If you don't hear anything, know this, you are called to go. There's a rule in the Armed Forces: "Always obey the last order you got until you get new orders from command headquarters." The last order I got in my Bible was GO!

Paul goes even further. He prefers that others get served before him. God puts an unchangeable, undeniable love in our hearts. And that love doesn't just stay within the borders of the United States, or in the borders of our denomination, or in the borders of our own church. But it is so large, and it is so explosive that it explodes everything that gets in its way with gentleness and power from the Holy Ghost.

Sure there are people that go to the ends of the earth that aren't Christians. In fact, the Mormon church sends their young people for two years of their lives to the mission field. Every single Mormon youngster goes for two years to the mission field. How come we can't even match that? How come we can't send our young people for six months? How come it is a special breed? But you're asking, "Keith, what about the lost in America?" Hey, don't worry. If God makes it clear to you to go, there will always be enough people, who won't obey the call, to stay around and witness here. Don't worry. You say, "But Keith, I need to keep my secular job and keep sending my $50 a month to World Vision. If I don't, who will?" Don't worry, there will always be enough people around that won't obey the call, that will send a check rather than their bodies as living sacrifices. There will always be enough people. Now, I am not saying that everybody that doesn't go is disobedient. I am just saying that about 99.99% are. That is what I believe. I've seen the world, folks. I've seen that it is lost, and there are billions of people over there that don't know God. Now either it is His fault . . . or it's ours.[5]

When our Commander gives us an order, we have only two choices, submit or rebel, obey or not. The Great Commission is meant for all of Abraham's Children, even as the Great Covenant and the Great Commandment were. Will we be obedient to Jesus even as He was obedient to His Father's love for the world? Every Christian must face the challenge of obedience to Jesus in light of His global plan. Are we followers of Christ? Or have we conveniently chosen which of Christ's commands we will observe and which we will treat as suggestions?

We do not need more insight in the Church; we need obedience to what we already know. James Hudson Taylor said, "The Great Commission is not an option to be considered but a command to be obeyed."

Mark Twain, in his funny way, understood our problem: "Most people are bothered by the passages in Scripture which they cannot understand; but as for me, I always noticed that the passages in Scripture that bothered me most are those which I do understand."[6] So many churches are clamoring for deeper insight and more revelation from God. There are whole movements that treat scriptural knowledge as though it is a mystery that only they along with the help of their prophetic guides can comprehend. If we are not hearing from God a fresh word, perhaps we should go back and examine whether or not we have been obedient to that which He has already revealed. (Disobedience brings blindness; obedience brings revelation! Deut. 28:15, 28) Revelation is for the obedient. Intimacy is for those who obey. (John 14:21, 23) We do not need some smooth talking, mystery-revealing prophet; we need churches full of obedience to His Great Command! Then God will release insight.

> *If you have My commandments and obey them,*
> *you love Me.*
> *And if you love Me,*
> *My Father will love you and I will love you*
> *and show Myself to you.*
> *If you love Me, you will do what I say*
> *and My Father will love you*
> *and We will come to you and live with you.*
> *(John 14:21, 23)*

Notes

1. Frank S. Mead, *Encyclopedia of Religious Quotations,* (London: Peter Davies, Ltd., 1965), p. 308.
2. Ralph D. Winter, "The Abraham Connection," (Pasadena, CA: U.S. Center for World Missions, 1995).
3. Edythe Draper, *The Almanac of the Christian World* (Wheaton, IL: Tyndale House Publishers, Inc., 1990), p. 722.
4. Vinita Hampton and Carol Plueddemann, *World Shapers* (Wheaton: Harold Shaw Publishers, 1991), p. 106.
5. Keith Green, "Keith Green Memorial Concert," (Lyndale, TX: Last Days Ministries, 1982).
6. Mead, *Encyclopedia of Religious Quotations,* (London: Peter Davies, Ltd., 1965), p 34.

seventeen

Where Have All the Pioneers Gone?

"You would believe in pioneer missions if your family were
part of an unevangelized people group."[1]
Norm Lewis

Try It; Maybe You'll Like It

I just returned from a missions conference. I have been told that there were several thousand in attendance. One young lady struck up a most disturbing conversation with me. When I asked her if she was considering going as a missionary, she responded saying, "Now don't get me wrong. I am a good Christian and all . . . I just want the good life."

Wave after wave of people walked by. Other than a handful of "extremists," people were uninterested in going. Well, that is not entirely true. Many were experts in short-term travel thrills and vacation adventures. One young lady had "done" five missionary trips totaling $8,000 in funds. Everyone seemed to want a short-term trip.

Who will go for the long haul? Who will lay down his own life and culture for the sake of Christ, His kingdom and the people sitting in the lands of darkness? One gentleman spoke of his time as a missionary pastor of a local Russian church for a year. Had he learned the language? No. Had he bonded with the people? Only superficially. Had he been Christ incarnate to them (living the life of God before them in a culturally relevant and sacrificial way)? Now his attitude was one of "done it, seen it, been there."

As I wandered around the conference I saw and heard this being advertised by several mission agencies who were also interested in getting people for the long term:

Where Have All The Pioneers Gone?

"Go on a short-term trip and try it. You will know, at least, if it is for you or not."

Since when has our decision been based on whether or not we will like it? Perhaps this is the same argument that makes repentance so unpopular. Maybe the revivals of old will never occur in our generation, so long as people allow their desires and comforts to dictate God. God desires to build the character and nature of Christ in us. If we are to be called *Christ*ians in truth, then our desires and obedience will inevitably be brought into conflict, and the necessary response must be, "not my will but Thine."

Historically, short-termers have made a dramatic impact on God's global advance. In the 1790's through the next fifty years, much of Africa was won by short-termers. With missionary fervor that has rarely been rivaled since, thousands of missionaries assailed this continent with the light of Jesus. Each went, knowing they had an average life expectancy of two years. They considered their lives as nothing compared to the riches of obeying their Christ. They were willing to lay their lives down as living sacrifices for the sake of Christ and those who had no hope without Him. Mothers and fathers hugged and kissed their children, knowing that eternity would be their next meeting. These were those who packed their belongings in their own coffins. The greatest Love had come to lay down His life again through these, His Body.

Rare Breed
C. T. Studd, in 1885, was a wealthy British sports hero, a cricket star. He was like the Tiger Woods of his day. He had money and fame, yet he gave it all away to follow Jesus! In response to critics who thought he was throwing away his life as a missionary to China he said, "Some wish to live within the sound of the chapel bell; I wish to run a rescue mission a yard from hell."[2]

When three pioneers of the Sudan Interior Mission, Walter Gowans, Thomas Kent and Roland V. Bingham, set out for the vast, unoccupied territory of the Sudan, they volunteered their lives, relying on Jesus to open their way. They went singing this song:

> For many years have Christians gazed, and then stood still, aghast, And said the dangers were too great, this field was closed fast. But Jesus' power shall break the bars and burst the gates of brass, The dark Sudan shall hear the name of Jesus.[3]

Within months, Gowans and Kent had died. Bingham, himself desperately ill, was forced to leave the field. Despite this early tragedy, in a few years, those graves were surrounded by churches. Before sailing for Africa, Gowans wrote of death:

Even death is not failure. His purposes are accomplished. He uses deaths as well as lives to the furtherance of his cause. After all, is it not worth venture? Sixty million souls are at stake.[4]

Bingham returned home, barely alive, but he rallied the troops for another assault on the heart of Africa. Today, south of the Sahara Desert, Africa is 50% Christian due to the dedication of pioneers such as Roland Bingham who said, "I will open Africa to the Gospel or die trying."[5]

The pioneer missionary to the Muslim world, Samuel Zwemer knew this passion, "The pioneer missionary, in overcoming obstacles and difficulties, has the privilege not only of knowing Christ and the power of His resurrection, but also something of His suffering."[6]

Take Malla Moe, for instance, who lived a long life of missionary service among the Zulus of South Africa. Arriving at a mission station she was asked, "Have you come on foot these twelve miles? Have you walked all the way?" "Oh no," she replied, "I have been running part of the way, and I have had the joy of leading sixteen souls to Christ." When Dr. T.J. Bach, her mission director, was visiting her, he suggested that she come home on furlough. She answered, "No, I am afraid that the board of directors would not let me go back again. If Christ tarries and I must die, I want to die among the Africans."[7]

James Hudson Taylor was the great missionary to China whose life and passion defined the inland missionary era for the Church. Until this time, mission agencies had been relegated to all the coastlands of the world. Taylor was not satisfied with just getting to the coastlands. He looked to the vast interior of China and saw the millions of people beyond the reach of the Gospel. He determined that no distance, no land, no government restriction could keep the Gospel from those peoples whom Jesus loved and for whom He died.

In Taylor's journals we see his heart regarding those who have never heard:

On Sunday, June 25th, 1865, unable to bear the sight of a congregation of a thousand or more Christian people rejoicing in their own security, while millions were perishing for lack of knowledge, I wandered out on the sands alone in great spiritual agony.[8]

On one occasion, Taylor was preaching in China and in the crowd one young man was looking and listening intently to him. Taylor was pleased that finally he was getting some results from his preaching, and at the end of his message, he gave the Gospel invitation. When this young man did not respond, Taylor pointedly asked him if he was interested in Jesus. The young man said, "No. I'm not really, but I'm very curious to know why you have buttons on your jacket." The Chinese had never seen buttons, and they did not understand what use they had. They were not accustomed to European dress. It may seem like a no-brainer for us in this day, but Taylor took the radical measure of saying, "Enough. I do not want my clothing to be a distraction and a stumbling block for people hearing the Truth of Jesus Christ." He abandoned western clothing for Chinese clothing, and this was considered outrageous by the other missionaries of the time. This man of God not only was methodologically a pioneer, but also broke new territory by going deeper inland than any missionary had ever gone.[9]

Where are They Today?
There are many missionaries today, but there are few pioneers. Where are the pioneers who reflect Paul's ambition to preach where Christ has not been named rather than to build upon another man's foundation? (Rom. 15:20, II Cor. 10:16) Instead, I mostly encounter an army of overseas administrators, educators, hospital workers, and builders. Where are the church planters that long to blaze the new trail? Where are the Harmon Schmelzenbachs who so desired to reach inland areas for Christ that he ignored health warnings and pressed in willing to die for the Gospel. The cost was much higher than his own death, yet at the grave of his first precious child he said, "If I had a hundred children, I would give them all for Africa."

I have met some pioneers, fervent in their call, but because their denomination does not work in their field of interest, they surrender their heavenly calling to earthly authorities. Most mission agencies and denominations started out as frontier, pioneer types, but over time they needed to maintain their successes. Just one generation later, most are involved in secondary activities. David Woodward, in the sixties, hit it on the nose when he said,

> Many missionaries go out with a desire to emulate this spirit of sacrifice, only to find themselves diverted from first hand contact with the unsaved. They find themselves so involved in the care of existing churches that they have little opportunity for pioneer evangelism.[10]

One of my missions students had just returned from over twenty years as a missionary in Africa. His heart broke as we began to talk of these issues. "I was willing to live in grass huts with dirt floors and take the Gospel into the hardest conditions, until I met the other missionaries. I discovered quickly that they were not living a life of sacrifice and pioneer ambitions, so soon I slipped into their model. Now twenty years later, I am reviewing my career and discovering that we were wrong."

I know of another missionary who is basically a stock room manager, sent out from North America under the title of missionary. He has had to on his own time, without official endorsement from His denomination, sneak off to the unreached tribes to the north and evangelize! Praise God that His Spirit still is calling us to pioneer. Pioneer missions is the manifestation of the Spirit of Christ. He was the one who refused to stay in one place, but pushed out to new areas and regions with the Gospel of the Kingdom. Jesus knew that this was the assignment of the Father. (Luke 4:43)

Jesus once told His disciples to "launch out into the deep." I believe that now is the season that our Master again tells us to launch out into the deep. S.D Gordon saw this when he wrote:

> The shore waters are largely over-fished. Out in the deeps are fish that have never had smell or sight of bait or net. Here, near shore, the lines get badly tangled sometimes, and committees have to be appointed to try to untangle the lines and sweeten up the fishermen. And the fish get very particular about the sort or shape of the bait. Some men have taken to fishing wholly with pickles, but with very unsatisfying results. The fish nibble, but are seldom landed apparently. And just a little bit out are fish that never have gotten a suggestion of a good bite.[11]

Heart of God Ministries' (HGM) first missionary was of this rare pioneer stock. David attended one of my seminars and was convinced that he needed to do more for missions, so he decided to sell his plasma to send money to support frontier missions. One day while giving his blood, God spoke to him, asking him to give more than his blood. God asked him to give his life as a pioneer missionary.

He came to our very first Boot Camp, and on the first day of class he asked me, "Where is the darkest place on planet earth?" I told him (specifics withheld for security reasons), and he said, "Then that is where I am to go." Today he is the leader of a team of missionaries
deep in one of the darkest places of the earth.

Another of our first missionaries literally auctioned off all of the family's belongings to afford the training and to go. They have the kind of heart, the same spirit of J.W. Ewen when he said, "As long as there are millions destitute of the knowledge of Jesus Christ and the Word of God . . . it will be impossible for me to devote my time and energies to those who have both."[12]

Missiological Triage
When God calls a person to go to the ends of the earth, Satan wars against the call. It is amazing how the pastor and church that should be encouraging a pioneer

calling actually do much to combat it. A close friend of mine and his wife both are clearly called to be missionaries, yet their pastor continually holds them back with pleas like, "Don't leave. We need you in the Children's Department just now." Isobel Kuhn, missionary to the Lhisu, heard this same tired line:

> Often, on furloughs, I have heard the impatient remark: "Why go to the foreign field? There is lots to be done at home here!" There most certainly is. And there are lots of Christians at home — are they doing it?[13]

People are people everywhere, and one soul is as valuable as another, so how do we explain the priority of the unreached? How can we say the frontiers deserve our time and energy and funds when we have neighbors who still do not know Jesus as their Savior?

M.A.S.H. was a popular television show based around a mobile medical hospital that served the U.S. military in Korea. One thing I learned from watching this show is something about *triage*. The ambulances would rush into the hospital, and the medics would lay the patients out on the ground. Doctors rushed out and quickly surveyed the wounded. They looked for the worst cases that needed the most urgent attention. For example, the man with a broken arm could wait, while the individual with the open belly wound needed to be treated immediately. This process is called *triage*.

Those doctors were not prioritizing an individual's value over another. They were simply recognizing who was in worse shape and needed more immediate attention. We need to have eyes of *triage* when we look at the world. We will find some people groups with access to the Gospel, and we will see others with some access to the Gospel. Then those who need our most immediate attention are those with no access to the Gospel.

Missionaries are not the men and women who take the Gospel to every person on planet earth. Pioneer missionaries cross new language and cultural boundaries that have thus far kept the Gospel out, to plant the seed of the Church. Then, with its own evangelists, the church planted will naturally grow, and believers will multiply. The goal of the frontier missionary is to give each tongue, tribe and nation the Gospel, then allow the planted church, like the mustard seed tree, to do the rest of the work of spreading out.

Which Way to the Front?

Now is not the time to rest on our laurel wreaths of conquest when half of the world sits in darkness. It grieves me that so much of our "missionary reading" is really all about what was done and what is being done in reached parts of the world. It hardly qualifies as missions any more. Yes, it is cross-cultural; yes, it is overseas, but it is not pioneer. Going overseas merely qualifies one as a tourist. Taking the Gospel to places it has not been makes one **apostolic!**

We love our success and continue to slap ourselves on the back for the sacrifices of the early pioneers and the fruit they bore. I know of one denomination that had at one time almost one third of its entire missionary force working in the country of Swaziland. Swaziland is at least 80% Christian.[14] This is hijacking the resources and personnel of God. He has set them aside to advance the kingdom, and we continue to go over the same ground. The Swazis should have been sending missionaries to Oklahoma City that only has a comparatively paltry 40% Christian population.

Robert Hall Glover stated it best:

> It is hard to understand how the soul of Christian youth is not filled with holy ambition, born of loving loyalty to Christ and strong compassion for lost and suffering multitudes, to dedicate their lives, with all their God-given talents and capabilities, to this greatest and noblest cause in all the world, that of "preaching the gospel in the regions beyond," where as yet the name of Christ has never been heard. Every "unoccupied" area and unevangelized tribe or community in the world today, nineteen hundred years after the Great Commission was given, is a sad reproach upon the fair name of Christ, and a shameful reflection upon the Church which professes allegiance to Him. God's words to Israel years after they entered the promised Land are truly applicable to His Church today with reference to the missionary "land of promise" (Ps. 2:8): "There remaineth yet very much land to be possessed . . . How long are ye slack to go to possess the land which the Lord God of your fathers hath given you?" (Josh. 13:1; 18:3) . . . We should take no satisfaction in the job half done, only take our past victories as evidence of ultimate victory!
>
> A missionary working on the borders of Tibet wrote these impressive words: "The eyes of Christians should turn as instinctively toward the lands closed to the Gospel in this missionary age as do the eyes of a conquering army toward the few remaining outposts of the enemy which withstand the victors and hinder complete victory, and without which the commander-in-chief is unable to close the campaign."[15]

We must let the passion of the frontiers engulf us, as it did the great missionary and father-in-law of David Livingston, Robert Moffat, "I've seen, at different times, the smoke of a thousand villages — villages whose people are without Christ, without God, and without hope in the world."[16]

Notes

1. Norm Lewis, *Priority One* (Orange, CA: Promise Publishing Co., 1988), p. 96.

2. C. T. Studd, *Some Wish To Live . . . Quotations From C. T. Studd* (Worldwide Evangelization Crusade)

3. David Brainerd Woodward, *God, Men and Missions* (Gospel Lighthouse Publications, 1964), pp. 37-38.

4. Ibid., pp. 37-38.

5. Vinita Hampton and Carol Plueddemann, *World Shapers* (Wheaton: Harold Shaw Publishers, 1991), p. 18.

6. Ibid., p. 119.

7. Woodward, *God, Men and Missions,* p. 95.

8. Marshall Broomhall, *Hudson Taylor The Man Who Believed God* (London: China Inland Mission, 1930), p. 117.

9. Ruth A. Tucker, *From Jerusalem to Irian Jaya* (Grand Rapids: Zondervan Publishing House, 1983), p. 176.

10. Woodward, *God, Men and Missions,* p. 94.

11. S. D. Gordon, *Quiet Talks On Service* (New York: Fleming H. Revell Company, 1906), p. 119.

12. Paterson, Ross, *Explaining Mission* (Kent, England: Sovereign World Limited, 1994), p. 20.

13. Isobel Kuhn, *By Searching* (Philadelphia: China Inland Mission, 1959), p. 120.

14. Patrick Johnstone, *Operation World* (Grand Rapids: Zondervan Publishing House, 1993), p. 516.

15. Robert Glover Hall, *The Bible Basis of Missions* (Los Angeles: Bible House of Los Angeles, 1946), p. 84.

16. Hampton and Plueddemann, *World Shapers,* p. 3.

eighteen

Names Demons Recognize

"His great heart cries out that we should win men and bring
them into the way of salvation. It is, thus, in fulfilling
our part of the covenant supreme [Acts 1:8] that
we satisfy the great **heart of God**."[1]
Edward Lawlor

What is Left to Do?
What is the task remaining for the Church, the heirs of Abraham's covenant? Have
we completed the Great Commission in getting the Good News to every nation?
Geopolitically — yes. Mongolia, a couple of years ago, was the last geopolitical
nation to have a church. Now they have one. But, remember, the term that our
Bibles translate as "nation" in the Great Commission is *ethne*. It has little to do
with geography or politics. It has to do with ethnic, linguistic and cultural groups.
John in Revelation describes it as "tongue, tribe, and nation."

Our best research indicates that there are approximately 6,000 ethne in the world
who have never heard about Jesus Christ.[2] Those 6,000 people groups represent
two billion individual souls with no chance to hear unless a missionary goes to
them. In China, where I am working — despite the amazing growth of the Gospel
among the Han Chinese — there are still over 400 languages and tribes without
access to Jesus!

For instance, in North Africa, which is predominantly Muslim, there is one
missionary for every two million people. If the situation were proportionally the
same in North America, there would only be 120 Christian workers and seven small
churches to choose from for the entire population of Canada and the United States.[3]
That is not enough for your city, is it? But that is the condition of the North
Africans.

For the people of The 10/40 Window, it is not simply a matter of them not having
responded to the Gospel. These people do not have access. It is the difference

between being lost in Wal-Mart and being lost in the Sahara desert. In Walmart you can ask a guard to help you out. Make a noise in a locked closet, and you will be found eventually. It does not matter how long these people yell and scream and look for relief; they cannot find it.

Remember God's favorite verse — the one He is so fond of repeating — "The earth shall be filled with the knowledge of the Lord as the waters cover the sea"? How do waters cover the sea? Is it piled high in the Atlantic and bone dry in the Pacific? Down around the capes the seas come together and even out the difference of about four or five feet. They are fairly even. Right now God's glory is not even. Afghanistan has over 80 people groups, and not a single one of them has access to the Gospel — a sea of unreached people in an ocean of unreached people groups with no access to the Gospel. The waters seem to be piled high in half the world and bone dry in the other.

Currently the Church sends about 8% of its missionary force to these unreached people groups. The other 92% are working primarily in places where 60% or more of the people consider themselves Christian.[4] Oswald J. Smith posed the most disturbing question in regard to the unreached, "Why should so few hear the Gospel again and again when so many have never heard it once?"[5]

Jesus and Paul: Names Demons Recognize

In Acts 19, some Jewish exorcists tried to expel a demon from a man. The demon responded, "Jesus, I know. Paul, I know, but who are you." (Acts 19:15) Often we think that the power over demons is in the correct order of our words, or even the use of the name, Jesus. These guys invoked the name of Jesus and the name of Paul, but to no avail. The demon beat them up. Beyond some "catch phrases," there must be the corresponding reality of our life. Why would the names of Jesus and Paul strike fear in demons, and why are their names recognized in hell? Because their passions, their time, their energy — their life -- was in complete agreement with God and His Kingdom expansion priorities. They were both uniquely ambitious to see the kingdom of darkness crushed by the advance of the Gospel. As a result, all of God's authority and power were resident within them.

In Luke 4:43 we see a little glimpse into the apostolic heart of Jesus. In the midst of great awakening in Capernaum, Jesus was healing people and casting out demons. People came from as far away as Decapolis to hear His preaching. There was great fervor and excitement over the message Jesus was preaching and the works He was doing.

After a whole night of ministry, Jesus sneaked off to get away to pray. The people could not find Him. They searched and searched. Finally, they found Him, and they begged Him to stay. (Luke 4:42) Maybe they said things like this:

"You just got here. What are you talking about leaving?" "I mean, I don't really get the Kingdom of Heaven stuff. Could you explain it again?"

"We've got a whole line up of these Gentiles coming to be healed. What are we going to do with them?"

"Did you know, Jesus, that the Romans are still in charge?" "The Governor of our region, he's sleeping with women."

"Did you know that our school system is messed up? Do you know what they're trying to teach our kids now?"

"You can't leave now, Jesus. Things aren't in order here." And you know what Jesus said?

> But He said to them, "I must preach the kingdom of God to the other cities also, because for this purpose I have been sent" (Luke 4:43).

God sent Jesus for a purpose, and here we see a little bit of this apostolic heart to go where He had not yet been, to continue to advance the Good News of the Kingdom of Heaven. We more often exemplify the spirit of those wanting to stay a long time in one region and get it totally fixed of all its problems, earthly and spiritual.

We all agree that Paul was a great missionary. You have to wonder, was Paul aware of some general commission that commanded "Go and preach the Gospel in unevangelized areas, and if you cannot go, send someone else?" No. He quotes Isaiah 49:6 as his Great Commission: "I will also give you as a light to the Nations, that you should bring My salvation to the ends of earth" (Acts 13:47). This was the commission of Jesus and the purpose of the Christ, but Paul understood clearly that Jesus' mission was also his. Paul understood that as the Father had sent Jesus, so Jesus was sending him. If Jesus could say *"I must preach the kingdom of God to other cities also, because for this purpose I have been sent,"* it would come as no surprise that Paul should declare,

> My ambition is to preach Christ where He has not yet been named rather than to build upon another man's foundation (Romans 15:20).

Romans

Our traditional understanding of Romans has been that it is an apologetic document used to expound on theological truths. Often when we study Romans, we focus on one word. We look at the word *propitiation* or the word *justification* for a month.

Names Demons Recognize

We get caught up in the mini-context of the word, taking a small theme of the passage and blowing it up very large like in a microscope, so as to examine it. Sometimes we need to back way up and look at the whole picture again. Let us look at the mega-context of Romans. For what purpose was it written? Most who interpret his writings and give commentary, are not qualified to do so, because they do not share his ambition. Paul was far more than an "ivory tower" theologian; he was a pioneer missionary.

To truly understand Romans is to interpret it within the context it was written. The key to understanding how the various themes of Romans all fit together is found in Romans 15:20-24:

> It has always been my ambition to proclaim the gospel where Christ was not known, so that I would not be building on someone else's foundation . . . I plan to do so when I go to Spain. I hope to visit you while passing through and to have you assist me on my journey there, after I have enjoyed your company for a while.

Paul was ambitious to advance the Gospel to regions beyond and was introducing himself to the Romans, so that they would support him in his ministry to Spain. In a very long sort of way, Romans is a missionary fund-raising letter! Paul was asking them to support him financially, materially, and with personnel, so that he could take the Gospel to the unreached region of Spain. This letter and all its theology can only be understood in the light of its missiological intent. This is a synopsis of the whole book of Romans:

Dear Church in Rome:

> Through Him and for His name's sake, we received grace to call people from among all the peoples . . . The truth about God is known to all instinctively. God has put this knowledge in their hearts. Since the earliest times men have seen the earth and sky and all God made and have known of His existence and great eternal power. So they will have no excuse . . . God will be the just judge of all the world. He will punish sin wherever it is found. He will punish the heathen when they sin, even though they never had God's written laws, for down in their hearts they know right from wrong . . . For we have already shown that all men alike are sinners. As Scripture says, "No one is good - no one in all the world is innocent." . . . Not one of them has any excuse. In fact, all the world stands hushed and guilty before almighty God . . .

Yes, all have sinned. All fall short of God's glorious ideal . . . . So God's blessings are given to us by faith as a free gift . . . That is what the Scriptures mean when they say that God made Abraham the father of many nations. God will accept all people in every nation who trust God as Abraham did . . . Remember what the prophecy of Hosea says? There God says that He will find other children for Himself (who are not Jews) and will love them though no one had ever loved them before. And the heathen of whom it once was said, "You are not my people," shall be called "sons of the Living God." . . . Anyone who calls upon the name of the Lord will be saved.

But how can they believe in Him if they have never heard of Him? And how can they hear about Him unless someone tells them? And how will anyone go and tell them unless someone sends him? . . . Remember that He came also that the Gentiles might be saved and give glory to God. That is what the Psalmist meant when He wrote; "I will praise you among the nations and sing to your name" . . . and the prophet Isaiah said, "There shall be an heir in the house of Jesse and he will be the King of the Nations; they will pin their hopes on Him." . . . So all the while, my ambition has been to go still farther, preaching where the name of Christ has never yet been heard, rather than where a church has already been started. I follow the plan spoken in the Scriptures where Isaiah says that those who have never heard the name of Christ before will see and understand. In fact, that is the very reason I have been so very long in coming to visit you . . .

I commit you to God who is able to make you strong and steady in the Lord, just as the Gospel says, and just as I have told you. This is God's plan of salvation for you Gentiles, kept secret from the beginning of time. But now as the prophets foretold and as God commands, this message is being preached everywhere, so that every ethne will have faith in Christ and obey Him. To God, who alone is wise be the glory forever through Jesus Christ our Lord. Amen.

Sincerely,
Paul

New Testament

The very context of the New Testament is pioneer church planting in a world full of unreached peoples. Often I have heard that really there is not much discussion and encouragement in the Epistles regarding missions. But saying the word missions is not necessary when the very context is missionary. The New Testament letters were written by frontier missionaries to pioneer churches. In fact, every book in the New Testament was written by a missionary. All the epistles in the New Testament that were sent to an individual were written to a convert of missionary endeavors. Every letter in the New Testament written to a church was sent to a missionary church plant. Of Jesus' twelve disciples, all became missionaries, all except the one who became a traitor. Most of the problems, which arose in the Book of Acts Church, were questions swirling around missionary procedure. It is impossible to be a student of the early church, Paul, and the New Testament without understanding that missions is at the core of the life of its author and intended reader.

Evangelism by Remote Control

In this modern world of technological wonder, some would tell us that the need for pioneers is over. You are encouraged to invest yourself in the pricey methods of radio and satellite evangelism. I remember watching one Christian television show brag about how, through their satellite broadcasts, there would be no unreached place left on planet earth. One Christian TV ministry claimed that they were the fulfillment of Mark 13:10, that the Gospel was now preached to every nation on earth. Sadly, very few of those nations spoke English, and sadly, few had satellite receivers. When Jesus said, "As the Father sent me, so send I you," it was more than about the task; it was also a commission to witness in like manner. He came in the flesh and dwelt among us. (John. 1:14) In Jesus, God was manifest in the flesh. (1 Tim 3:16) He then commissioned us to do the same, to the ends of the earth, laying down our lives in the flesh, that through our clay pots the glory of God might be revealed. It will take a whole army of people who will identify with the unreached, go and dwell among them, leave their father's home and their people and go to the land that God shows them. Missions by remote control is not the answer. Missions without the person is not good enough.

Dr. Samuel Zwemer, a pioneer missionary to the Arab world, was once speaking to a crowd of people in a hospital waiting room. A Bedouin, who had traveled over 500 miles to receive treatment, pulled Dr. Zwemer aside and said,

> I understand all you told us, because I have seen that man myself. He lived in my own country years ago. He was a strange man. When people hurt him, he did not seek revenge. He looked after the sick, the prisoners, and those in trouble. He seemed to think one man as good as another. He used to take long trips in the broiling sun to help others. He was just what you said.[6]

It took some doing, but Dr. Zwemer learned that the individual the Arab Bedouin was speaking of was Peter Zwemer, his own brother, who had been a missionary in Arabia years before. Though he died after only a few years of ministry, he had revealed Christ through his own life of love for others.

I read one critic of radio ministry that said it was an ungodly form of evangelism, because it uses airwaves to travel, and after all, we know that Satan is the prince of the air. That is foolishness. Radio ministry is a great tool to support and assist the missionaries in the flesh, but never a replacement. Only through the pioneer missionary who learns the language and lives among the people will the truth of Jesus be revealed to those who are currently blinded by the god of this world. Only His apostles that learn the culture and way of life will be Christlike in methodology. For thirty years, Jesus became one of us, that we might fully comprehend the Good News. If we do not become one of them, they will never fully hear nor fully understand the Good News we have been entrusted to tell.

John R. Stott wrote:

> We believe so strongly in proclamation that we tend to proclaim our message at a distance . . . We appear to be giving advice from the security of the shore to men who are drowning. We do not dive in to help them. We are frightened at the thought of getting wet, and besides, this implies many dangers. We forget that Jesus did not send His salvation from heaven; He visited us in our humanity.[7]

Timothy McVeigh's Verdict

My daughter learned about capital punishment, while Timothy McVeigh was on trial for the bombing of the Oklahoma City Federal Building. She saw him on television. As Jessi looked at his face, she turned to us and said, "He doesn't look like a bad man."

Many years ago another man who was under sentence of death was found at the last moment to be innocent. A messenger was dispatched with a pardon from the governor and told to deliver it to the place of execution. Thinking that there was time, he lingered in route and stopped for a rest and food at a wayside inn. Thoughtlessly he fell asleep. Waking suddenly, he realized his terrible error. Wildly he dashed across the countryside, renewing horses at every post. At last, he dashed up the Courtside Square yelling loudly calling out the message of pardon that he had brought. Alas, he was too late. A minute before, that innocent man had been put to death. Could the messenger ever forgive himself for that crime?[8]

The Word of God is clear that all men already stand condemned. We are all guilty and deserve our death sentence. No one is innocent, all are guilty. Our and their only hope of salvation is in Jesus Christ. Paul says, "Whosoever calls on the Name of the Lord shall be saved" (Rom. 10:13). Then he goes on to enlist every

Christian with a chain of logic from which none are exempt: "How shall they call on Him in whom they have not believed, and how shall they believe on Him in whom they have not heard and how shall they hear without a preacher, and how shall they preach unless they are sent?"

If you are a Christian, then one day in your past you received that desperately needed pardon signed in the blood of the Lamb. That same pardon that was life to you is available to every condemned soul. All are under this sentence of death. You, Christian, are part of the delivery team. Are you stopping for rest and relaxation? Have your own comforts lulled your spirit to sleep. Do you find that there is very little real urgency in your efforts?

Many wrongly treat their commission to deliver the freeing message of pardon as an occasional activity. Its obedience competes with life's pleasures and pursuits. In today's business of maintenance and accumulation, there is very little room for our immediate neighbor let alone the unreached in India.

But our commission is not a "free time" endeavor. It demands our all. Like wild riders across the land, rushing to rescue the condemned, so must our lives, priorities, time and energies be conformed to the urgency of the moment.

Tim McVeigh had advocates who pled for his life. But the unreached have none to care for their souls. No one begs for mercy; no one cries out for their lives. We stand back and do nothing, leaving them strapped to their deathbeds. Pardon is granted but not delivered.

Unless we are doing all we can to get the Gospel to the unreached peoples of our world, we are in essence content to let their deaths go unhindered. Missions is not about rolling bandages and sending care packages in our free time, though that is of great encouragement. It is about a no-holds-barred struggle over these still trapped in dunengeons of darkness with the executioner at the door. We have no more excuses. The pardon is in your hand, and the command of Christ still stands to take it to the ends of the earth. Will you obey with abandon or will you toy with their eternal destinies. What is the verdict?

Notes:

1. Edward Lawlor, *The Covenant Supreme* (Kansas City, MO: Beacon Hill Press, 1952), p. 51.

2. Frank Caleb Jansen, *A Church for Every People,* Adopt-A-People Clearinghouse, 1993.

3. Perspectives Office, USCWM, Pasadena, CA.

4. Bill and Amy Stearns, *Catch the Vision 2000* (Minneapolis: Bethany House Publishers, 1991), p. 135.

5. Oswald J. Smith, *The Challenge of Missions* (London: Star Books, 1995), p. 38.

6. Earl C. Wolf, *Choice Illustrations* (Kansas City: Beacon Hill Press, 1965), pp. 54-55.

7. G. Christian Weiss, *God's Plan, Man's Need, Our Mission,* (Lincoln: Back to the Bible Publications, 1971), p. 124.

8. A. B. Simpson, Missionary Messages (Camp Hill, PA: Christian Publications, 1987), p. 58.

Witness!

"We are never closer to God than when we share
His heart for the unevangelized."[1]
Patrick Johnstone

"What we want is a heart in communion with the **heart of God**, the
heart of Christ, and that will surely be a heart for souls."[2]
C.H. Mackintosh

Interesting Timing

How long after Jesus' resurrection did the disciples wait before the Holy Spirit came upon them? A week, three weeks, months? What was God waiting for? It is no coincidence that the Holy Spirit came seven weeks after the resurrection. (Acts 1:3) Why not six or eight or two? After Jesus died and was raised from the dead, about seven weeks passed before the Holy Spirit came. You have to wonder about the timing of that. Was it that they got holy enough, and they prayed hard enough, and then, suddenly God said, *"Okay, you deserve it now"*? No. There was something else going on when the Holy Spirit came:

> And there were dwelling in Jerusalem Jews, devout men **from every nation under heaven**. And when this sound occurred, the multitude came together and were confused, because **everyone heard them speak in his own language**. Then they were all amazed and marveled, saying to one another, "Look, are not all these who speak Galileans? And how is it that we hear, each in our own language in which we were born? Parthians and Medes and Elamites, those dwelling in Mesopotamia, Judea and Cappadocia, Pontus and Asia, Phrygia and Pamphylia, Egypt and the parts of Libya adjoining Cyrene, visitors from Rome, both Jews and proselytes, Cretans and Arabs — **we hear them speaking in our own tongues the wonderful works of God**."

Witness!

> So they were all amazed and perplexed, saying to one another,
> "Whatever could this mean?" (Acts 2:5-12)

What was God waiting for? He was waiting for the celebration of Pentecost where He could inaugurate His Church. The purpose of the Holy Spirit (as Jesus stated) is underlined by the timing of His arrival. What a birthday it was! Boom! The Holy Spirit came on them. They went out speaking in many different languages, and the people were saying, "I'm hearing everything in my own language." From where had these people come? They were from all over the known world. They were God-fearers, Gentiles that had converted to Judaism, maybe people whose forefathers back in Nebuchadnezar's time heard of Daniel or Shadrach, Meshach and Abednego and were convinced that their God was the real God! Many of these Godfearers still lived in Damascus or even as far away as India.

This international collection had gathered in Jerusalem for the great Feast of Pentecost, which by the way, was the Feast of First Fruits. It was not the Feast of the Harvest Gathered, but the Feast of First Fruits. If you remember from Chapter Ten, they would take the first fruits from the vine and wave it before the Lord and say, "More, Lord! We're not satisfied! We want more!" That was the Feast of Pentecost, and this was when God decided to introduce His Church. It was not the finished product; it was the First Fruits of this glorious international Church of Jesus Christ. They were gathered to hear it in their own language, and three thousand were won in that day! The Church was born in a glorious blaze!

Paul, the frontier missionary, throughout his life kept running into people who knew a little bit about Jesus. There was a church in Asia and in Rome. Where did they hear it? Who was out ahead of Paul? It is likely that these churches were born here on the Day of Pentecost.

Purpose of the Holy Spirit

> But you shall receive power when the Holy Spirit has come
> upon you; and you shall be witnesses to Me in Jerusalem, and in
> all Judea and Samaria, and to the end of the earth (Acts 1:8).

Jesus talked of the power of the Holy Spirit as being given in the context of going to the nations — missions. The Holy Spirit's power is given for a very special purpose: "to be My witnesses in Jerusalem, Judea, Samaria and to the end of the earth."

The purpose for the Holy Spirit's arrival is to advance the Gospel among the nations. Many churches want the Holy Spirit's blessing without the attached responsibility of being a witness to the nations. He will only come in apostolic, Pentecostal power to vessels through which He knows He can bless the nations.

If we want revival in our churches, and if we want a fresh indwelling of the Spirit in our churches, then we need to know to whom the Spirit comes and why He comes. Perhaps herein lies our answer to why He has not blessed our churches with a fresh anointing.

Many will find my defining the Holy Spirit as coming in power for the Great Commission to be offensive to their idea of the Holy Spirit as their Comforter. When He is called the Comforter, that does not necessarily mean that He is here to sympathize with us. There is a famous painting of an English king poking his soldiers in the back with his sword, encouraging them into battle. Underneath are the words, "King George the First, comforting his troops." The Old English word *comfort* meant to encourage, to provoke, to stir.[3]

Along with empowering the Church, the Holy Spirit simultaneously convicts the world of sin. The idea is that the two will meet somewhere in the middle. The two purposes will not miss each other. The Church will go out, and the lost will be drawn in. Whether your doctrine is Entire Sanctification or the Baptism of the Holy Spirit — whatever term you want to use — this is significant. Entire Sanctification or the infilling of the Holy Spirit is not the end in itself. It is a means to an end. Completion of the Great Commission is the end, and the infilling, the empowering of the Holy Spirit, is a means to that end.

You have probably heard that the Holy Spirit is a lot like electricity. He will not go in where He cannot go out. The Holy Spirit is not going to fill a vessel through which He cannot flow and become a blessing to others. Many are in search of power, a revival of blessing of sorts, some kind of a Pentecostal experience, but they want the blessing without the attached responsibility.

Martus
John G. Paton, the pioneer missionary to the South Seas relates this story:

> Amongst many who sought to deter me, was one dear old Christian gentleman, whose crowning argument always was, "The cannibals! You will be eaten by the cannibals!" At last I replied, "Mr. Dixon, You are advanced in years now, and your own prospect is soon to be laid in the grave, there to be eaten by worms; I confess to you, that if I can but live and die serving and honoring the Lord Jesus, it will make no difference to me whether I am eaten by cannibals or by worms."[4]

The Greek word that we have translated *witness* (in Acts 1:8) is really *martus,* the word from which we get our English word *martyr. Witness* is a somewhat less than powerful translation. In our understanding, witness means when we knock on someone's door and then a few seconds later breathe a sigh of relief -- no one is home. "Whew!" That is our idea, but God is saying, *"The Holy Spirit is coming on you with power, so that you can be my martus! You can be my witnesses unto death to the ends of the earth."* Anybody want to step forward and receive the power of the Holy Spirit?

There are two kinds of *martus.* There is the daily dying that we have to do. I do not believe that one can really be a *martus* in a physical, blood spilling out on the ground sort of way, unless you have been a *martus,* dying to your own desires. If we have not died that death, forget the other grand and glorious executioner's block. This is the reason the power of the Holy Spirit is given.

James Calvert was on his way to ministering to the cannibals of Fiji Island, when the captain of the vessel tried to dissuade him. "You will risk your own life and the lives of those who sail with you if you go among such savages." James calmly replied, "We died before we came here."

The pioneer is one who knows that his life is not his own, and with power he is convinced that to die is gain, to live is Christ. (Phil. 1:21) As good soldiers of Christ, pioneers were ready to go and lay down their lives in the service of their King. Marshal Foch knew how to win, "Battles are won by teaching soldiers how to die, not how to avoid dying." Nate Saint, one of the five who died while trying to reach the Agarunas, prophetically said, "The way I see it, we ought to be willing to die. In the military, we are taught that to obtain our objectives, we have to be willing to be expendable. Missionaries must face that same expendability."[5]

We Are the Body of Christ
The first time that Jesus came in the flesh, He died for the lost of the world, gladly laying down His precious life that others might have true life! Now that He is enfleshed in you, I wonder what He wants to do? "Hopefully He learned better . . . maybe he will try the subtle route now to evangelism, perhaps take it easier through me..." No. He is the same yesterday, today and tomorrow. James Hudson Taylor lived this truth: "The missionary spirit is the Spirit of Jesus, the Spirit of the Incarnation *and the Cross.*"[7]

We are in the business of saving others, not saving ourselves. While suffering on the cross, the crowd mocked Jesus because He "could not save Himself." That was the goal! The whole point of the Christlike walk is not to save our self but to lay our life down in the salvation of the world. "He who saves His life will lose it, but He who gives His life for My sake and the sake of the Gospel will find it."

Everywhere we see the Church growing, it is because someone laid down his or her life in blood, sweat and tears. When we look at the phenomenal growth of the Church in China, we see a correspondence to the beloved martyrs. There is no way around the law of the exchanged life, which is the expansion of the

Church. E-mail and faxes are not the church growth secret we have been waiting for. The law is exemplified by Christ who said that a grain of wheat must die, or it will remain by itself; but if it dies, then it becomes many. Paul also repeated this principle when he said, "We bear death in our bodies that you might have life." (2 Cor. 4:12) It is the law of an exchanged life. The peoples of our world must have their Calvary before their Pentecost. By 150 AD, Tertullian already understood, "The blood of the martyrs is the seed of the Church."[7]

Heart of God Ministries, the mission agency with which I serve, does not guarantee that we can ever get people out of frontier areas. It is still a dangerous job, this thing we call frontier missions. Even though the doors are "closed," in that governments and religious leaders do not welcome us, the windows are still open. He did not say, *"Go if the doors are open, and you are warmly welcomed by the governments, given a missionary visa and legal protection to preach."* Jesus said, *"Go."* The apostles did, in the face of government opposition and executions. They went, opposed by the religious leaders, to whom they said, "Whom shall we obey, God or man?" (Acts 5:29)

How sad that so many churches and mission agencies have lost the passion for obedience to Jesus at all cost. In doing so, they have relegated themselves to only those countries that will roll out the red carpet for them. It is sad also for those who still sit in lands of deep darkness, who are prisoners of governments and religions that do not welcome missionaries. Shall we just hope and pray that the next generation is more "open" to the Gospel?

Why are there still unevangelized areas of the world? Because they are hard to evangelize. I tell you, all the easy places to evangelize are finished. The only places left to take the Gospel are the hard ones, the ones that will cost us blood, sweat and tears. Throwing money at it will not work. Instead, like the military assaults of old, we must throw ourselves in what some would call reckless abandon to penetrate these last, unwelcoming bastions of demonic darkness. Where are the young people of Christendom that so understand the heart of their Savior and are likewise moved by compassion for the multitudes that they do not count their own lives as worth anything, but will gladly risk all for the sake of the imprisoned souls among the unreached?

Holy Sacrifice

Late one night a concerned lighthouse keeper watched as a violent storm erupted at sea. Suddenly the seasoned keeper saw the faint SOS of a ship in distress. Grabbing his raincoat, he looked at his young apprentice and commanded, "Let's go!"

Horrified, the apprentice retorted, "But, sir, if we go out there, we may never come back."

> The old keeper of the lighthouse paused and put his
> hand on the young man's shoulder. "Son" he responded, "we
> have to go out. We don't have to come back."[8]

"Jesus said, 'Greater love has no one than this, that one lay down his life for his friends'" (John 15:13). The story of missions is full of illustrations of men and women who sacrificed their lives, so that others might come to know Him who is Lord of all, including us. History tells us that while wild beasts in the amphitheater were tearing apart some Christians, other Christians were in the balconies witnessing to their faith in Christ.

Sacrificing one's life for the sake of Christ and others is not limited to those specially called to ministry and service. During the war in the Pacific, three young, Christian men came to their chaplain the evening before the scheduled landing on one of the enemy occupied islands. Casualties would be heavy, and everyone involved knew it. The chaplain was hardly prepared, however, for the purpose of their visit.

> "Chaplain," one of them began, "we came, because we want
> you to pray with us. We know that tomorrow many of us will
> die in the battle. Casualties are going to be heavy. But, chaplain,
> we are not afraid. We know Jesus Christ and are prepared for
> death. But we also know that there are a lot of men who are not
> prepared to die, and for whom death will mean judgment and
> not eternal life in Christ. We want to pray that if some must die,
> and if it please God, we are ready to give up our lives so that
> some others may live and have yet another opportunity to hear
> about Jesus. Will you pray with us?"

> The next day all three of these young men lost their lives in the
> battle. One cannot but wonder whether there were any among
> the hundreds whose lives were spared, who did not know the
> Lord but had another opportunity to hear of his grace, because
> three young men were willing to give up their lives so that they
> might hear.[9]

C. T. Studd had this same Holy Spirit of sacrifice. When the China Inland Mission asked for volunteers to go and minister in a province in China which had just had terrible riots and violence against foreigners, chasing them all out and burning all foreigners' property, Studd volunteered. When he, after having to come home because of health reasons, passed by a church with a poster that read, "Cannibals Need Missionaries," he laughed and then went inside to volunteer. He lived to be an old man, but He was a *martyr* the whole time. He never took the comfortable, easy or popular road. He said, "If Jesus Christ be God and died for me, then no sacrifice can be too great for me to make for Him."[10] Do you not hear the ring of apostolic Christianity in those words?

When John Wesley encountered the refreshing, selfless sacrifice that characterized Moravian missionaries, he exclaimed, "Oh when will this brand of Christianity the world fill?" Paul, the Apostle, stated his brand of Christianity with these words: *". . .nor do I count my life dear to myself, so that I may finish my race with joy, and the ministry which I received from the Lord Jesus . . ." (Acts 20:24).*

Notes

1. Patrick Johnstone, *The Church Is Bigger Than You Think* (Pasadena: William Carey Library, 1998), p. 281.

2. C.H. Mackintosh, *The Great Commission, Miscellaneous Writings, Volume IV* (New York: Loizeaux Brothers, 1898) p. GC-85-86.

3. Ray Comfort, *Springboards for Powerful Preaching,* (Bellflower, CA: Living Water Publications, 1993), p. 44.

4. Vinita Hampton and Carol Plueddemann, *World Shapers,* (Wheaton: Harold Shaw Publishers, 1991), p. 20.

5. Hampton and Plueddemann, *World Shapers,* p. 19.

6. Ibid., p. 90.

7. Franks S. Mead, *Encyclopedia of Religious Quotations,* (London: Peter Davies, Ltd., 1965), p. 300.

8. David Shibley, *A Force In The Earth,* (Lake Mary, FL: Creation House, 1989), p. 65.

9. Richard R. DeRidder and Roger S. Greenway, *Let the Whole World Know,* (Grand Rapids: Baker Book House, 1988), pp. 121-122.

10. Hampton and Plueddemann, *World Shapers,* p. 19.

twenty

Ignorance Isn't Bliss; It's Hell

"Oh for a fresh, clear, arresting vision of the whole world
to break upon the Church of Christ, constraining all
Christians to lift up their eyes and look out unselfishly
beyond their own narrow boundaries and local interests,
and share their **Savior's burden of heart** for the souls
of all mankind!"[1]
Robert Hall Glover

"There shines the glorious truth that a poor, self-convicted,
broken-hearted, penitent, though hell-deserving
sinner gives joy to the **heart of God**."[2]
C.H. Mackintosh

Love as Hot as Hell!
The whole warehouse shook as a few miles away the horrible bombing of the Oklahoma City Murrah Federal Building sent shock waves around the world. Suddenly, getting my car's oil changed was no longer the important issue of the hour.

As the day revealed the death and destruction, it took a personal toll. Just one week before, on the same morning at 9 a.m., I had stood in that Social Security office looking out the big picture windows facing the street. Now, all the people I dealt with, those who helped me were dead.

Oh, to rescue them, physically, if possible. Though I barely met them, I would gladly claw through the rubble with my bare hands to free them. But I know they are dead. They are facing eternity.

Even those who escaped will someday die. There really is no difference between those who survived and those who didn't. The saving efforts of the rescuers wasn't a permanent fix; it was a temporary save. There used to be a time when the central focus of our Christian talk was saving the pagan's soul. To snatch sinners from hell was a holy fervent passion.

Ah, but there is a fresh wind blowing. 'Tis the wind of education and evangelical sophistication. In this enlightened trend, the Church is trying to move more toward ministries that emphasize the whole man. In the name of holistic ministry, we try to minister to people's physical, emotional and social needs. We frame it and hang it in our church offices.

Temporary Salvation.
But where has hell gone? It has faded into the distasteful recesses of fuzzy gray. We have forgotten the terrors of hell, and it has caused our love to grow cold (Matt. 24:12) — our love for Jesus and our love for the lost.

Perhaps we have forgotten the condition of our own soul? Have we forgotten, or perhaps never known, the salvation of our God? He has literally saved us from hell, snatched us from the fires. Hell not only becomes a natural motivation for evangelism, but first and foremost imparts to us deep gratitude and worship. Perhaps our embarrassment or lack of belief in hell is the reason our passion for Jesus is so low. We don't know from what we have been saved. He who is forgiven much, so will his love be. (Luke 7:41-47)

Paul, the Apostle, states that he would rather go to hell than to let those who are lost go there. Paul so strongly identified with the lost and their eternal fate that he could not brush it aside casually, but he was burdened down with the weight and desperation of hell. He was driven to the greatest form of love, the willingness to lay down his own life. It was not a program that his church installed to witness to the neighbors, nor was it a faith promise offering from which he could walk away, claiming to have done his part. It was a life consumed by the urgency of people's need to be rescued from hell.

I see most Christians as having removed their lives from the discomforting notion of hell, and I can understand why. Of all the things Jesus talked about, I wish this were not one. To ignore hell is much more palatable and culturally suitable. Trumpet temporal salvation, and you will win the world's admiration.

Yet, we cannot afford to ignore hell. For in as much as we give in to that convenience, to that same degree we will see our love turning cold. It is our understanding of hell that fans the flames of our love for Jesus. It is the reality of hell that heats our passion to save the lost. Both loves will only be as hot as our vision of hell.

Is there a Hell?

A more terrifying scene is hard to imagine. There were people being sawn in two, babies being eaten, tongues cut out, women disemboweled and others roasted slowly. I was in Chang Hwa, in the middle of the island of Taiwan. They were not real people just animated likeness. It was kind of an horrific version of Disney's "It's a Small, Small World" or the "Pirates of the Caribbean." Level after level, the terrors of the after-life were displayed before our eyes. This vision of the terrors of eternity is not the result of some over zealous Christian missionary, but part of a Buddhist temple. Here they are trying to show the penalty of sin. If you are a bad mother, then this is your torture in hell; if you are a robber, then you will suffer this fate; if you had an abortion . . . The Chinese know that sin carries a penalty of torment and payment. What they do not know is that the penalty of their sin has been paid by someone else. They do not know that this hell can be avoided, and Jesus has been provided as a substitute. The unreached know that hell exists.

The Bible is clear that hell exists, so we are not going to discuss whether or not hell exists. There is a popular trend in the world to vote hell out of existence or to try and diminish what the scripture says about hell — where the worm never dies, where there is unquenchable fire, where there is weeping and gnashing of teeth, outer darkness, fire and brimstone. Many people, even those whom we would call mainline denominations or conservatives, are uncomfortable with hell. None of us are comfortable with hell. If there were a doctrine in scripture that we could vote to get rid of, I would be the first one in line to vote against hell. But scripture has not changed. When we look at the New Testament and the twelve times that hell was specifically taught, eleven of them are by Jesus Himself. If Satan fails to march us to hell, he will try to work us up over non-central, secondary, even unimportant issues, while the rest of humanity marches to hell.

Will the Unreached Go There?

We need to ask the question in regard to all men everywhere. Are men without Christ lost? I know many that are convinced that people are basically good and just need a bit more education, yet somehow a look at history would challenge this idea. Down in Mexico, they are proud of their ancient civilizations; they had calendars that were so much more accurate than ones currently in use. They had complex government and civic life. They had an infrastructure matching Rome's, yet they were monstrous in their brutality. In our day, taking no prisoners is merciless. In their day, taking prisoners was the height of mercilessness. They sacrificed all that were captured to their bloodthirsty gods, first opening the prisoners' chests and removing their beating hearts. What do we say about such violence and horrors? They need some more education on tolerance?

If that were only in the distant past, we could excuse it away. In our day, we have had millions butchered under such evil as Hitler and the Nazis. The Germans were one of the most highly educated and "enlightened" people of their day. What do we say of their murderous cold-blooded cruelty? They had a bad day?

Today, we have the evil of ethnic cleansing in what was once Yugoslavia, and the murder of Hutus and Tutsis in Rwanda and Burundi. Our world doesn't need more education. People are lost. Jesus said He came into the world to *seek and save that which is lost.* Do you think that Jesus was mistaken to call men lost? They are not just lost in eternity; they are lost right now!

Regarding hell and man's lost condition, both presently and eternally, we really do not believe scripture. We yell at people who are in darkness, telling them they shouldn't be doing what they are doing, as though they are people in the light. But the truth is that they are in darkness, and given over to evil, and apart from rescuing them from the kingdom of darkness, there is no hope. Jesus said, "I am the Light of the world; whoever follows me will no longer walk in darkness, but will have the light of life" (John. 8:12). Not only did He claim to be The Light, He stated clearly that without Him, people are struggling in darkness. Apart from Christ, people are in death and darkness, and Jesus is their only escape to life and light. Jesus came "to give light to them that sit in darkness and the shadow of death" (John 1:79). John 1 is perfectly clear: Jesus was the true light, and this light gave life to men. It shines in the darkness, and the darkness doesn't overcome it. Jesus is the only light in a sea of darkness, and only those who follow Him have this light which is life!

Romans is clear. There is no room for the closet Universalist in this powerful book. A.T Pierson, the founder of the Christian Missionary Alliance, wrote:

> For one, I hold we must either give up the inspiration of the Word, or accept the lost condition of the world. The epistle of the Romans deals with these very questions and leaves no standing room for any candid doubt, unless we deny that Paul spake under the moving of the Holy Ghost. We can scarcely read the introductory chapter of that masterly epistle, which is logic on fire, without observing a fearful indictment of the whole pagan world from idolatry and iniquity. Yet he does not hesitate to affirm that they are WITHOUT EXCUSE, because that when they knew God, they glorified Him not as God.[3]

J. Hudson Taylor encountered the same unbiblical thinking in his day:

> "I meet a good many people who say to me, I cannot believe that the heathen are lost, because they have not heard the Gospel; and I fully agree with them. I believe they are lost, because they are now in sin and go on in sin. It is not a delusion as to whether

people will be lost. We are lost, because it is a state of nature. The unconverted are lost already, but they can learn that Jesus Christ came to seek and to save, not those who are in danger of being lost, but those that are lost."[4]

The lost people groups of the world did not start out as lost. In other words, they at one time knew of God, but in subsequent generations wandered far from that knowledge. (Rom. 1:21-23) Secondly, they did not lose all knowledge of God. They had enough pointers and clues that had they really searched for Him, they could have found Him, for He is not far from any of us. (Romans 1:20 and Acts 14:17) Also there is the human conscience, which works as an ally of God, in convicting us of wrong. (Romans 2:14-15)

If a man is finally condemned, it will not be because he refused to believe in Jesus Christ or because he did not hear the gospel. It is because he failed to live up to the light that he had. Yes, if someone walked perfectly regarding his conscience and the light he had received, he would be saved. But no one does that. This is where so many useless philosophical debates should end. The Word of God is the measurement by which we must gauge our thinking. Romans clearly states that "no man is righteous, not even one." (Rom. 3:10) "All have sinned and fall short of God's glory," and all are equally condemned, having nothing to do with the presence or absence of the Gospel. Jesus is the Good News to a condemned world that He has borne the wrath due us and has provided a way to the Father! James Hudson Taylor said that in fifty years of being a missionary in China he never met anyone who claimed to live up to the light that they had. Moral failure is a universal phenomenon.

When missionaries first went to Greenland, one of the first converts said,

> It is true, we were ignorant heathens and knew nothing of God or of a Savior; and, indeed, who should tell us of Him until you came? But thou must not imagine that no Greenlander thinks about these things. I myself have often thought a boat, with all its tackle and implements, does not grow into existence of itself, but must be made by the labor and ingenuity of man; and one that does not understand it would quickly spoil it. Now, the meanest bird has far more skill displayed in its structure than the best boat; and no man can make a bird. But there is still a far greater art shown in the formation of a man than any other creature. Who was it that made him? I bethought me that he proceeded from his parents, and they from their parents; but some must have been the first parents; whence did they come? Common report informs me they grew out of the earth; but if so, why does it not still happen that men grow out of the earth?

And from whence did this same earth itself, the sea, the sun, the moon, the stars arise into existence? Certainly there must be some being who made all these things; a being that always was and can never cease to be. He must be inexpressibly more mighty, knowing, and wise, than the wisest man. He must be very good, too; because everything that He has made is good, useful, and necessary for us.[5]

But did that intelligent, insightful Greenlander need Jesus? Yes, for as Paul cried, all humanity agrees: *"That which I desire to do I cannot, Oh who will save me from this body of death? Thanks be to Jesus!"*

While wrestling with the question of the condition of the heathen apart from Christ, a mentor of mine helped me with this illustration: What use is it to talk of other possible methods of salvation? It is like being in a burning building and wondering if someone on the 20th floor could possibly survive if they opened the window, tied all their bed sheets together, crawled as far down as they could on their own and then dropped to the pavement below? Could they? What foolishness to pause and muse on this at all. Should we not in concern for their life be rushing up and yelling, "Fire! Fire! The fire exit is over here! Come this way; it is the way to safety!"? Yet often this is the sort of discussion that many use to justify their lack of concern and justify their selfish inactivity on behalf of those who have never heard of Jesus. Scripture tells us that the lost are without God, without life and without hope. How bad off are they? The unreached themselves don't really know. You and I clearly don't have a good grasp. Only Jesus really knows how desperate the situation is, and He tells us to *go!*

The question whether the heathen really need Christ may be answered by the counter question: Do we need Him? John R. Mott answered:

It is not necessary that we go to scripture, or to the ends of the earth, to discover our obligation to the unevangelized. A knowledge of our own hearts should be sufficient to make plain our duty. We know our need of Christ. How unreasonable, therefore, for us to assume that the nations living in sin and wretchedness and bondage can do without Him whom we so much need even in the most favored Christian lands.[6]

The intensity of my desire to give them Christ is in proportion to my own awareness of their need. Past generations heard much about the lostness of those without Jesus, but our generation prefers to meditate on the blessings of Jesus and not on the consequences of being without Him. If we truly believe that Jesus is "life," we can not avoid concluding, that being without Christ is death.

He who says to the wicked, you are righteous, peoples will
curse Him. Nations will abhor him. But to those who rebuke
the wicked will be a delight, and good blessings will come upon
them (Proverbs 24:24).

"O Jesus, am I responsible for any of them? Would some of them be
shining and shouting in glory today instead of weeping and wailing in
hell, if I had gone to them, or sent [someone to] them? How much, O
how much am I personally responsible?"[7]

All Roads Lead to Fuji[a]

Well, no, actually not all roads lead to Fuji. I have driven many roads, all my life,
hours upon hours. I have had cars die under me, wheels burst and engines blow.
I have traveled roads in blazing summer and through white-out blizzards. I have
slipped off the road, hit other cars, been stopped by the police, but I have never
been to Mount Fuji. I think that I could drive my whole life and never find Mount
Fuji. You know why? Because all roads don't lead to Fuji.

Some people think that perhaps God has revealed Himself through other religions.
In many colleges today, you can actually get a degree in Comparative Religions
— comparing the similarities between religions. Though I don't doubt that God
could have spoken to others in other religions, and indeed there may be true
precepts and many admirable qualities in other religions, that does not mean that
they lead to salvation.

I am not talking double talk. We are all in agreement that Judaism is inspired by
God. We even consider their scriptures to be from God. But all faithful followers
of Judaism must repent and follow Jesus. Peter stood up in the second chapter of
Acts and talked to fully sincere and devout Jews. Was their sincerity enough to
save them? No. Peter told them they must repent and be baptized in the name of
Jesus!

> Nor is there salvation in any other, for there is no other name
> under heaven given among men by which we must be saved
> (Acts 4:12).

Who is the *we*? God fearing, law obeying Jews. But can the law save? No. Paul
and Jesus agreed with Peter. Paul says the law can not free the Jew; it only stands
to condemn. Jesus demanded that the religious leaders trust in Him, otherwise
they would die in their sin. If this great world religion of Judaism, which is totally
inspired by God cannot save, then what religion can? For even the Jew, repentance
and believing in the finished work of Jesus is necessary for salvation. How much
more will it be necessary for the Buddhist or the Hindu? No matter how good

precepts are within a religion, it cannot save, for there is salvation in no other name under heaven!

Jesus said:

> "I am the door. If anyone enters by Me, he will be saved, and will go in and out and find pasture" (John 10:9).

> "I am the way, the truth, and the life. **No one comes to the Father except through me**" (John 14:6).

Proper Motivation?

It is every parent's nightmare to have a child missing. J. Oswald Sanders relates his experience:

> When our daughter, Debbie Jean, was six, she disappeared one day. We searched everywhere for her — the other houses nearby, the shopping center, the schoolyard. I remember walking up and down a little dirt road calling, "Debbie Jean," and fearing the silence. Two hours later she showed up and told us she had gone with a friend to a candy store and then on to the friend's house. After the thunder, lightning and tears had passed, I reflected: During those two hours that my little girl was missing, there were books that I had to read, letters that I had to answer, telephone calls I had to make, planning I had to do — but I could think of only one thing: My little girl was lost. I had only one prayer, and I prayed it a thousand times, "God help me to find her." But how often, I asked myself, had I felt the same terrible urgency about men who are lost from God?

> What led Jesus to weep over Jerusalem? Or Paul to cry, "Woe is me if I preach not the gospel"? Or John Knox to pray, "Give me Scotland or I die"? Or Henry Martyn to land in India saying, "Here let me burn out for God"? Or George Whitefield to cross the Atlantic thirteen times in a small boat to preach in the American colonies? Or the aristocratic Lady Donnithorne of our own generation to go into the forbidden precincts of Hong Kong's "walled city" to bring the healing of the gospel to the pimps and prostitutes? Or Jim Elliot and his friends to stain a river in Ecuador with their blood to reach an obscure Indian tribe?

> They were gripped with a tremendous conviction that without Christ men really were lost in a deep and eternal way.[8]

When we compare the two great missionary centuries, the first and the nineteenth centuries, we will find a common understanding that we seem to have forgotten. The missionaries in both were strongly convinced of the reality that people were lost apart from Christ. Their desire to rescue them from hell was a central motivator to their missionary ambition. Hell makes us so squeamish, that some of my good friends have labeled hell as an improper motivation for missionary service. I agree that the pure desire to glorify Christ is great! I know that the motivation of loving God through obedience is proper. But to deny that the concern of Paul and Jesus was not also grounded in their love for mankind is naive. We have yet to recapture the apostolic passion of Paul, and Jesus, and James Hudson Taylor and a whole host of others, if we forget hell. Mr. J. Hudson Taylor affirmed, "I would never have thought of going out to China had not I believed that the Chinese were lost and needed Christ."[9]

William Hesslop, an early missionary to Korea, said,

> Brother, sister, I want to tell you calmly and quietly, I am resolved, God helping me, to stretch this poor body of mine across their pathway to a burning hell, if perchance some may stumble over it and land in a happy Heaven. I am resolved, God helping me, my time, my talents, my money, my strength, my all, shall be thrown between them and their hopelessness and helplessness here and hereafter if perchance some may hear the gracious invitation, accept and be saved. Beloved, what will you say? What will you do?[10]

A woman missionary in Iran explained, "None but women can reach (Muslim) women . . . so we have a solemn duty in this matter that we can not shift. The blood of souls is on our skirts, and God will demand them at our hands."[11]

"I continually heard . . . the wail of the perishing heathen in the South Seas," John G. Paton declared, explaining why he volunteered — over a hundred years ago — to go out as a missionary.[12]

Thy Brother's Blood

The following is taken from Amy Carmichael's book, *Things as They Are: Mission Work in Southern India.* It is easy to see why it caused such an uproar in the western Christian world. For many in the early 1900s, missions was considered a distasteful necessity requiring careful discussion. Amy broke this delicate mold. Here she mentions "tom toms." When someone died, these drums beat all night. On one sweltering India evening, the drums of death awakened her to the spectre of millions perishing without Jesus.

> The tom-toms thumped straight on all night, and the darkness

shuddered round me like a living, feeling thing. I could not go to sleep, so I lay awake and looked; and I saw, as it seemed, this:

That I stood on a grassy sward, and at my feet a precipice broke sheer down into infinite space. I looked, but saw no bottom; only cloud shapes, black and furiously coiled, and great shadow-shrouded hollows, and unfathomable depths. Back I drew, dizzy at the depth.

Then I saw forms of people moving single file along the grass. They were making for the edge. There was a woman with a baby in her arms and another little child holding on to her dress. She was on the very verge. Then I saw that she was blind. She lifted her foot for the next step . . . it trod air. She was over, and the children over with her. Oh, the cry as they went over!

Then I saw more streams of people flowing from all quarters. All were blind, stone blind; all made straight for the precipice edge. There were shrieks, as they suddenly knew themselves falling, and a tossing up of helpless arms, catching, clutching at empty air. But some went over quietly, and fell without a sound.

Then I wondered, with a wonder that was simply agony, why no one stopped them at the edge. I could not. I was glued to the ground, and I could only call; though I strained and tried, only a whisper would come.

Then I saw that along the edge there were sentries set at intervals. But the intervals were too great; there were wide, unguarded gaps between. And over these gaps the people fell in their blindness, quite unwarned; and the green grass seemed blood-red to me, and the gulf yawned like the mouth of hell.

Then I saw, like a little picture of peace, a group of people under some trees with their backs turned toward the gulf. They were making daisy chains. Sometimes when a piercing shriek cut the quiet air and reached them, it disturbed them, and they thought it a rather vulgar noise. And if one of their number started up and wanted to go and do something to help, then all the others would pull that one down. "Why should you get so excited about it? You must wait for a definite call to go! You haven't finished your daisy chain yet. It would be really selfish," they said, "to leave us to finish the work alone."

There was another group. It was made up of people whose great desire was to get more sentries out; but they found that very few wanted to go, and sometimes there were no sentries set for miles and miles of the edge.

Once a girl stood alone in her place, waving the people back; but her mother and other relations called and reminded her that her furlough was due; she must not break the rules. And being tired and needing a change, she had to go and rest for awhile; but no one was sent to guard her gap, and over and over the people fell, like a waterfall of souls.

Once a child caught at a tuft of grass that grew at the very brink of the gulf; it clung convulsively, and it called — but nobody seemed to hear. Then the roots of the grass gave way, and with a cry the child went over, its two little hands still holding tight to the torn-off bunch of grass. And the girl who longed to be back in her gap thought she heard the little one cry, and she sprang up and wanted to go; at which they reproved her, reminding her that no one is necessary anywhere; the gap would be well taken care of, they knew. And then they sang a hymn.

Then through the hymn came another sound like the pain of a million broken hearts wrung out in one full drop, one sob. And a horror of great darkness was upon me, for I knew what it was — the Cry of the Blood.

Then thundered a voice, the voice of the Lord. "And He said, "What hast thou done, the voice of thy brother's blood crieth unto me from the ground."

The tom-toms still beat heavily, the darkness still shuddered and shivered about me; I heard the yells of the devildancers and weird, wild shriek of the devil-possessed just outside the gate.

What does it matter, after all? It has gone on for years; it will go on for years. Why make such a fuss about it? God forgive us! God arouse us! Shame us out of our callousness! Shame us out of our sin![13]

"Don't Worry Be Happy"

I played golf recently. I was not any good. That night a friend of mine joked with me that golf was for "fat preachers." His humor stung, because I knew He was right.

Now don't get bent out of shape over the specifics of golf or engage in any discussion about recreational activity vs. workaholics. Let me continue. I knew that I was getting to be a "fat preacher." Slowly I have succumbed to the pleasures available all around me. Eating at a slightly more expensive restaurant, "relaxing" after a day of work with mindless sitcoms or challenging my office mate to another computer game.

Few have room to point a finger at me and say that I am slothful and lazy, for even our Christian society finds this behavior normal and even classifies it as "healthy." Yet I point my own finger at my heart and flesh, and even today I am in a period of repentance and reconsecration to Jesus and His life.

Jesus said, "My yoke is easy," but it is still a yoke of work, not "easy," as in "easy chair." Jesus said, "My burden is light," as in the "momentary light afflictions" Paul suffered. I see nothing in the life of Jesus, nor the Apostles, nor the saints who have followed, that reflects a life of ease — rather, that of careful urgency. James Hudson Taylor's life reflected this passion, "Would that God would make hell so real to us that we cannot rest."[14]

I sense that in my spirit a subtle deception has taken place through the intoxication of my own pleasures and saturation of the culture around me. Instead of hearing my Master's cry, "Redeem the time for the days are evil," I sing the anthem of our flesh: "Relax, eat, drink, be moral and merry."

But unlike you and me, God is very much in a hurry and casts aside everything that weighs Him down and entangles Him from His salvation mission. Through 2 Peter 3:9, we hear God crying that He is not willing that any should perish. Yet we happily fill our time with pursuits that summarize our wanton careless use of time, while millions perish destitute of any knowledge of the salvation in which we so happily bask. Jesus is urgent in His command to GO and proclaim freedom for the captives from the penalty, from the pleasure, from the power of sin and finally from the presence of sin.

Do we not recognize the terrible urgency of peoples' need? Are we so lacking in love that we are content to see them slip into eternity without Jesus? Do we not see the urgency of the Father anxious to save His children from their terrible predicament? We can muster up no urgency for them. Rather, in its place stands an urgency for our television program or our self-fulfilling activity of pleasure, like my seemingly innocent game of golf. I am not talking about work for work's sake, but diligently giving ourselves to the work of the Gospel for Christ's sake, offering up ourselves as living sacrifices to Him, considering nothing our own, be it a $15 green fee or a fifteen minute break.

"A student once asked C. H. Spurgeon if he thought the heathen who had never heard the gospel would be saved. The great preacher answered, "It is more a question of whether we, who have the gospel and fail to give it to those who have not, can be saved."[14] Dear friend, may God forgive us for our careless consideration of each hour and restore a passion for Him that will reflect in our urgency for the lost.

> Oh! for a heart that is burdened!
> Infused with a passion to pray;
> Oh! for a stirring within me;
> Oh! for His power every day.
> Oh! for a heart like my Savior,
> Who being in an agony, prayed.
> Such caring for others, Lord, give me;
> On my heart let burdens be laid.
> My Father, I long for this passion,
> To pour myself out for the lost
> To lay my life down to save others
> "To pray," whatever the cost.
> Lord, teach me, Oh teach me this secret,
> I'm hungry this lesson to learn,
> This passionate passion for others,
> For this, blessed Jesus, I yearn.
> Father this lesson I long for from thee
> Oh, let Thy Spirit reveal this in me.
> Mary Warburton Booth

Notes

a. "All roads lead to Fuji" is a commonly used phrase to refer to the belief that all religions lead to God.

1. Robert Hall Glover, *The Bible Basis of Missions,* (Los Angeles: Bible House of Los Angeles, 1946), p. 194.

2. C.H. Mackintosh, *The Great Commission, Miscellaneous Writings, Volume IV* (New York: Loizeaux Brothers, 1898) p. GC-18.

3. William Heslop, *Missionary Tidings,* (Greensboro: The Golden Rule Press, 1880's or 1890's), p. 46.

4. Ibid.

5. Rev. Elon Foster, *New Cyclopedia of Prose Illustration,* (New York: T.Y. Crowell, 1877), p. 384.

6. David and Naomi Shibley, *The Smoke of a Thousand Villages,* (Nashville: Thomas Nelson, Inc., 1989), p. 69.

7. Heslop, *Missionary Tidings,* p. 18.

8. J. Oswald Sanders, *How Lost Are the Heathen,* (Chicago: Moody Press, 1972), p. 17.

9. Vinita Hampton and Carol Plueddemann, *World Shapers,* (Wheaton: Harold Shaw Publishers, 1991), p.16.

10. Heslop, *Missionary Tidings,* p. 11.

11. Hampton and Plueddemann, *World Shapers,* p. 4.

12. Rev. James Paton B. A. The Story of John G. Paton, (New York: American Tract Society, 1902).

13. Amy Carmichael, *Things As They Are: Mission Work in Southern India,* (Dohnavur Fellowship, Morgan and Scott, early 1900's).

14. Sanders, *How Lost Are the Heathen,* p. 80.

twenty one

The End

"There is no better way to measure the self centeredness in the Church than the lip service that we give to the **heart of God** concerning those who are living in total darkness."[1]
Dr. James L. West

What is Taking Him so long?

A Christian from England was in Sudan, relaxing in the afternoon when the sun beat down the hottest. An old and weathered sheik came to him, asking a question.

"Do you know Jesus, the prophet?"

"Yes," replied the Christian.

"Well," the old man pressed, "is His coming soon?"

"I do not know."

The Muslim kept asking intently, "Is Jesus coming in the next few months, or is his coming after this year?"

The Christian replied, "God alone knows. I don't, but I do know Jesus is coming again."

Then his curiosity got the better of him; he asked, "Why are you wanting to know?"

The Muslim looked deep into the eyes of the Christian, nodded and spoke, "This is why I have asked you. I need you to describe what Jesus is like. For if he should walk by me in this desert, I would be able to recognize Jesus' face and then be able to correctly welcome him."[2]

How long did that old man look for Jesus? How long did He examine each new visitor to his region hoping it may be Jesus? How many are there today that still look and search and wait? Many trapped under governments of tyranny still await the justice of Jesus. One may wonder: "If God is so interested in establishing righteousness and justice on earth, then why doesn't He just come back and do it?"

The End

The nations wait for the justice of His law. Why does He not come back and give it? I will tell you why. He is waiting. For what?

> The Lord is not slack concerning His promise, as some count slackness, but is longsuffering toward us, not willing that any should perish but that all should come to repentance (2 Peter 3:9).

Why is He waiting? Because He is patient with us, waiting for us to come to repentance. The passage then goes on to describe what the Day of the Lord will be like. In verse 12, Peter makes this startling conclusion that all Christians should be:

> "...looking forward and hastening the coming of the day of God . . ." (vs. 12a).

We are to look forward to the Day of the Lord. Some of us watched those movies in the seventies and early eighties that depicted the tribulation with Christians running for their lives and heads being chopped off. Because of that, many hope the Day of the Lord never comes. But I do look forward to it. Why? Because He will give perfect justice to the nations. There will be no more evil. We look forward to that day, and what else? We are to "hasten its coming." Your version may say, "speed its coming" or "hurry it along."

This cannot be right! The return of King Jesus has nothing to do with me personally. Isn't it dependent upon events that are going to happen in Israel? His return is on some sort of cosmic timetable. It does not have anything to do with me, right? Ah, but it does. It has less to do with who is shot in Israel, than it has to do with you. This verse simply implies that Jesus is waiting for us to do something! Here is some blazing insight that you will not hear on "Prophecy in the News." You are part of the timetable of God. You are the trigger that starts the end time events. "Look forward to the day of His return and hurry it along." How do we do that?

Scripture is very clear. Let us look at Matthew Chapter 24. Here the disciples asked Jesus when He was going to come and establish His Kingdom, and Jesus replied, "You're going to hear about wars and rumors of wars, famines and earthquakes and all sorts of things.But the end is not yet. These are just like birth pangs."

My wife has had four children now. They were all natural childbirths, two of them at home, and so she is very aware of what birth pangs are. She felt every one of them, and I vicariously watched and felt them all. Honestly. I slept for days after it. It took a lot out of me.

Women, you know what birth pangs are about. They get longer and harder and closer together. The harder and longer and closer they are to each other, the closer the baby is to coming. Finally, they come one on top of another and the baby arrives. Now, no woman is foolish enough to cry out in the midst of a contraction, "Oh that's the baby." No, you endure the pain for the joy that will be yours afterwards, holding the baby. No woman says the birth pang is the baby. So, Jesus is saying, "You're going to have wars and rumors of wars and all these things, but they're birth pangs." They are not the end. Do you want to know what the end is? The next verse:

> And this gospel of the kingdom will be preached in all the
> world as a witness to all the nations (ethne), and then the
> end will come (Matthew 24:14).

This is scripture. I am not messing around with your mind here. This Gospel will be preached to all ethne, and then, and only then, will the end come. This is what the Word of Jesus says. His return is predicated on our completion of this task. The Great Commission was not optional, but a specific command to be obeyed. It is not refutable.

When we finish the job of getting the Gospel to all nations, only then will He return. If you are looking for something to happen in Jerusalem to trigger His return, just forget it, because He is not going to come back until this is done. Do you know why? Because He is not going to be a liar on that day when we get to heaven and we look around and say, "Not bad. You got 95% of the nations." No! Every tongue, tribe and nation will be standing before the throne in front of the Lamb, clothed in righteousness only provided by the death and blood of Jesus Christ (Rev. 5:9)! Therefore, He is waiting for us to obey and for them to repent and receive Jesus Christ. Maybe the Great Commission was indeed the Great Commission — something that He indeed wants us to accomplish — not something with which just to busy ourselves until He decides to come back some day.

Why are we so far from fulfilling the Great Commission? We are just like those people in the Tower of Babel. When it gets right down to it, we do not want to go. I meet many people who come to me and say, "When I was twenty, God called me to go. But, well, my denomination required that I have a degree," or "I married the wrong person, and he didn't want to go." These people are sometimes very bitter people. If God calls you to go, find a way to obey Him.

If you are retired, now you are able to go. The thing that is most respected on earth is age — not in North America, but if you have white hair or no hair, you will have a hearing in many places in the world. They honor your hoary head. It is not too late to go. Maybe God has given the Americans the idea of retirement, so that they can go ahead and go. It is never too late to be obedient to His Great Commission.

The End

Days of Noah

> Therefore, when they had come together, they asked Him, saying, "Lord, will You at this time restore the kingdom to Israel? And He said to them, "It is not for you to know times or seasons which the Father has put in His own authority. But you shall receive power when the Holy Spirit has come upon you; and you shall be witnesses to Me in Jerusalem and in all Judea and Samaria, and to the end of the earth (Acts 1:8).

So much of the Christian community, the leaders, the magazines that are out there are spending time on this exact same question that the disciples wanted to know back there in Acts. "When is it that you are going to return and establish your Kingdom on earth?" Jesus basically says, *It's none of your business, but here is your business: be My witnesses to the ends of the earth.*

So many of the "prophetic" community have for so long claimed that all the scriptures that set forth the conditions and world events necessary for Christ's return are fulfilled. Then why has He not yet returned? This alone should cause us to question whether or not all the conditions have indeed been met. Is there any wonder, with thousands of people groups and 2.1 billion people locked behind these prisons of culture, who have no access to Him as Savior, that he is not willing to return as Judge?

> But as the days of Noah were, so also will the coming of the Son of Man be (Matt. 24:27).

We are told that just as it was in the days of Noah, so shall the end times be. What were the days like? Evil and awaiting God's judgment. But in His mercy He preserved animals of every kind under heaven. He gathered them in His ark of protection. Only when this task of mercy was complete was the bowl of judgment poured out on the earth.

So it will be in these last days. The ark of God's salvation is still available. There is coming a day when it will be shut and no man can enter, but until then, He is gathering worshipers from all the peoples of the earth. (Matt. 13:39) Over and over God emphasizes His concern for ALL nations. His parables are replete with analogies to the nations. All the birds of the air can find rest in the branches of the Kingdom of Heaven — all the animals are brought into the ark of safety — all the kinds of fish are brought in by the dragnet of the Kingdom. (Matt. 13)

Now, before you think God is into collecting us into some sort of zoo or like some adolescent trying to get "the whole set,"[3] Jesus is showing us His heart's passion that goes beyond some sort of isolated tribal deity to a true love for every ethne! Perhaps the illustration of the ark is so simple and profound that up until now it has evaded our attention.

Memory Verse of Hell

If God is delaying His return and judgment until all nations have heard, then it is easy to understand why every boardroom in hell has Matthew 24:14 plastered on the wall: "And this Gospel will be preached in all the world as a witness to all the nations, and then the end will come." My friend and missions mobilizer, Phil Bogosian, calls this the Memory Verse of Hell.

If there is a boardroom in hell, this verse is plastered up on the wall there. Satan points to it and says, "Remember this!" Satan is time paranoid. What concerns Satan about this verse is "the end." The end means to him . . . the end. All that Satan has is time. He is time paranoid.

> The devil has come down to you, having great wrath, because
> he knows that he has a short time (Rev. 12:12).

The activity that shortens his time is the thing that enrages him most. The shorter it is, the angrier he gets. He militates against anything that shortens his time. In Matthew Chapter 8, Jesus had just calmed the raging storm on the Sea of Galilee, and as He and the disciples got to the other side, two demon-possessed men came running out to them. The demons in these men were so violent that no one could pass by them on that road. When these demonized men saw Jesus, this was their reaction:

> What have we to do with You, Jesus, You Son of God? Have
> You come here to torment us before the time? (Matt. 8:29)

Do you hear the fear in their voices? They are saying, "What have we done to warrant your coming to us now? It's before the time." What time are they talking about? The time of judgment. The time will come when the angels will indeed be judged by the Son of Man and will be cast into the lake of fire. That is inevitable. It is going to happen, but until that time, they can rule and reign, and it seems they can do whatever they want to on earth. Here they encountered Jesus, and they were screaming out, "Have you come to judge us before the time?" They were time paranoid. Why? Because time is all they have. When it is over, it is over.

Satan will have as much time as he wants, so long as he keeps the Gospel out of every ethne. He is going to resist the missionaries. It is going to be a life and death struggle to get the Gospel into these dark regions. It is warfare. That is why the simplicity of the Salvation Army hymn is a breath of fresh air, "The devil and me, we don't agree. I hate him and he hates me."[4]

The End

The other thing that Satan will do is to turn you off to missions. Have you ever been to a missions prayer meeting? Does anybody show up? Is it any wonder that missions is considered boring? We have to practically bribe people to come to missions events. Our missions committees have to do all kinds of marketing to get people excited. I have been in those meetings. The discussions go something like this: "Let's surprise the people. Let's not let them know this conference is really about missions. Let's call it a "celebration!"

We have to work hard to get people interested in missions, when this is the very reason God has left us on earth. The Church has no reason to exist except for the advancement of His Kingdom into areas it has never been before! Other than that, go home to heaven. You have nothing more to do here. Missions is the reason you are here, and Satan is going to keep you bored. He is going to make you think that missions is some inconsequential little side issue that is in competition with every other program of the Church, when in reality it is the *only* program of the Church!

Missions is the reason we live. The minute the Church gets on her knees, the minute the Church sells out to advancing the Gospel into these dark areas, Satan is done. Your personal world will always take up your time. Your personal world will always take up your money. Your little dreams, desires and worries will always totally occupy your life, unless you make a specific effort to say, "No, I'm going to go beyond my own life and lay it down, die to it, that I might give my life as a ransom for others."

As long as Satan can keep the Church distracted from this task, as long as he can keep in his control many nations and peoples of the world, he has time. Why is missions boring? Why is it so hard to pray for missionaries? Why is it that though we in North America are one of the richest societies in the world, only a pitiful 4% of our income is spent in missions and of that only 1.3% is given to reach the unreached?[5] The reason is Satan will throw everything he has at us to resist getting the Good News to these last people groups that need to hear. As soon as we begin to pray for laborers to be sent out into His harvest fields; as soon as we go, in obedience to His command, into His harvest field, that is the world, and bring in this harvest that is ripe in our generation, it will be "the end of the age." (Matt. 13:39)

Can We Finish the Great Commission?

Jesus has given us overwhelmingly greater resources than we need for the task. The issue is: will we continue to spend them on ourselves, or will we follow the Leader and lay down our lives that others might be saved?

It amazes me that though Jesus Himself, recently risen from the dead, was speaking to the disciples (You would think that the disciples would have been eating up every word that came from His mouth.), and though Jesus "opened their minds to understand Scripture . . . that repentance and forgiveness of sin might be proclaimed to all nations" (Luke 24:45-47), they did not understand it. For years, they did not understand it. Acts 11 has those wise men of God just then exclaiming, "Well then, (Surprise! Surprise!) God has granted the Gentiles also the repentance that leads to life." Hello! Where were they when Jesus told them years ago?

But is this not us? All of Scripture resonates with God's global passion. It is everywhere, but somehow, our minds filter it out. This is what it sounded like to the disciples: "The Son of Man should suffer and die and rise on the third day and that repentance and forgiveness of sin should be preached . . . blah, blah, blah." Somehow, the weight of this information must get past our ears and into our heart and life. Not just mental assent or faith that it is so. It must translate into action. As James says, "He who knows the good he ought to do, but does not do it sins" (James 4:17).

Why is it that we are so far from fulfilling God's design for the world? One reason is that we have not opened ourselves to the full force of the missionary message of Scripture. We are so caught up in the glitch (sin) and its resolution that we never get on with the further activity of God. Why? We do not see well. God gives us clear revelation of His character, purpose, activity and will for us . . . but we seem to deliberately wear dark shades with blinders, focusing on our own small, self-oriented world. Meanwhile, the world God loves is lost, and we are all dragging Him to our Christian ball game in our comfortable pew. Jesus said, "My food is to do the will of Him who sent me . . . and to finish His work" (John 4:34). Will we be about our Father's business? Will we finish His work?

The Titanic

It seemed a silly premise for a movie. Surely no one would want to go to a movie with such a predictable end. I was wrong. It was a blockbuster.

An interesting revelation regarding the Titanic is the tragic fate of those in third class. They were locked below deck as soon as the ship began to sink, so they would not get in the way of the more privileged classes. There was only enough room in the lifeboats for the wealthier passengers. The sad fact is that nobody cared. No one went down and freed them from their prison of death. As the great Titanic sank down, only the screams of the rich could be heard. Those in third class died without a sound, out of sight.

Some enjoy the debate; "If a tree falls in the forest and no one hears it, does it make a sound?" My question is, "If a person dies from among the unreached and no one knows their name, does it matter?"

The End

A whole generation of individuals from among the unreached peoples will go down without ever having a chance to hear of Jesus. The entire "third class" world will slip into a Christless eternity without someone opening the gate of their imprisonment and setting them free, while those of us from the more privileged class take our time getting to our own boat of safety.

Like those third class passengers, the world awaits the message of salvation. Over three hundred years ago John Elliot visited the Natick Indians. There they asked him how it was that even though the English had already been in the country for a considerable time, they had so long neglected to instruct the natives in the knowledge of God and why the English had not sooner imparted what they professed to consider so important. "Had you done it sooner," they said, "We might have known much of God by this time, and much sin might have been prevented, but now some of us have grown old in sin!" What answer would satisfy his question?[7]

In 1840, another chief from the Manitoulin Islands begged for missionaries to be sent to his people, "We have heard that our brothers who are near the white settlements have received the Great Word. We've heard that the Great Spirit has told the white man to send the Great Word to all His children; why does He not send it to us? I have been looking many moons down the river to see the missionary's canoe, but it has not come yet."[7]

Another African chief said to David Livingston, "All my forefathers have passed away into darkness without knowing anything of what was to befall them; how is it that your forefathers knowing all these things, did not send word to my forefathers sooner?"[8]

From all four corners of the planet we hear the cry, and what shall we say in answer? Proverbs 24:11-12 solemnly commands us,

> Deliver those who are being taken away to death. And those who are staggering to the slaughter, O hold them back. If you say, "See we did not know this", Does He not consider it who weighs the hearts? And does He not know it who keeps your soul? And will He not render to man according to his work?

Don't stand back and let them die! Don't try to disclaim by saying you did not know about the unreached. For God who knows all hearts knows yours, and that you knew. Not only will He give to each according to what they have done in rescuing the perishing, but also the converse is true. He will render to each according to their lack of work.

Somebody Forgets

A little fellow, of a very poor family, in the slum section of one of our large cities, was induced to attend a mission Sunday School. By and by, as a result of the teacher's faithful work, he became a Christian. He seemed quite bright and settled to his new Christian faith and life.

Someone, surely in a thoughtless mood, tried to test or shake his simple faith in God by a question. He was asked, "If God loves you, why doesn't He take better care of you? Why doesn't He tell someone to send you warm shoes and some coal and better food?"

The little fellow thought a moment, and then with big tears starting in his eyes, said, "I guess He does tell somebody, *but somebody forgets.*"[9]

Isobel Kuhn, in her book *Nests Above the Abyss*, wrote of a Lisu tribe of thousands of people:

Some of them heard this wonderful doctrine was being preached out in Chinaland, and a little party made the trip of two or three days journey to that missionary lady and asked her to come to tell them also. *That was ten years ago.* Ever since then, that lady (now over sixty years of age) has been trying to find someone to go to those Lisu, and up to this date no missionary has ever been resident among them. (Several made trips at various times, and report that the district truly is there and the Lisu number thousands.)

Ten years they have waited. Do you think that when they called for gospel messengers, *God* did not respond? It could not be. He gave His most precious Son that *all* might know and receive eternal life. I think that *man* did not respond. It costs something to leave loved ones and the comforts of civilization. I believe that *each generation* God has "called" enough men and women to evangelize all the yet unreached tribes of the earth. Why do I believe that? Because everywhere I go, I constantly meet with men and women who say to me, "When I was young I wanted to be a missionary, but I got married instead." Or, "My parents dissuaded me," or some such thing. No, it is not God who does not call. It is *man* who will not respond! "My flock became meat to every beast of the field, because there was no shepherd, neither did my shepherds search for my flock, but the shepherds fed themselves, and not my flock." (Ez. 34:8)[10]

> The restless millions wait the light
> Whose coming maketh all things new.
> Christ also waits, but men are slow and late.
> Have we done what we could? Have I? Have you?[11]

Leave Them Alone
They're Happy the Way They Are
These words have haunted missionaries all over the world. While my family dined with some very "comfortable" relatives, one, in an enlightened and educated way, informed me of the unreached peoples' "true condition:" "They are happy the way they are."

We must have all read the same rose-colored anthropology novel of a utopian tribal group whose hell began at the hands of a missionary. The reality of the dark terrors that have stalked our world's tribal societies is unknown: the daily fear of evil spirits, the bondage of a long and growing list of taboos, the endless cycle of revenge killings and the hopeless finality of death. These are all the horrors of a society without the Good News of Jesus, who is Life Eternal, who provides victory over the spirits and writes His laws on their hearts, empowering them to love their enemies.

I know that it would be inconceivable for us to say about a starving child, "Leave her alone, she is happy the way she is." We all understand and can to some degree identify with the reality of hunger and the physical devastation it brings. But, we evidently must not believe in the spiritual starvation of these tribes, or we could never think for a moment that they are happy." The essence of starvation is that unless we get food to them, they perish. Are we content to let them stand, dead in sin, hushed and guilty before the one just and holy God, imprisoned and enslaved by the god of this dark age and the corruption of their own understanding? How can we leave them alone?

Perhaps, unlike hunger, we are unaware of our own desperate need for Jesus. We do not feel the pangs of our own emaciated spiritual condition enough to have desperate compassion for those without any access to the Bread of Life. How different was the Apostle Paul's cry, "God, I would gladly suffer the fires of hell if that would save my brothers." (Rom. 9:3)

The scriptures tell us that the islands wait expectantly for His laws and that Jesus is The Desire of All Nations. Even in our real world, it is not an uncommon story for tribal villages to seek out the Gospel of the Kingdom. Some, prior to the missionaries' arrival, have already built a church building in anticipation of the Good News. Others have been known to send delegations in an attempt to purchase missionaries for their own village.

The sad truth is that there are just not enough people willing to go and lay down their lives that others may have the Bread of Life. The sad truth is that the nations are not happy the way they are, but it is we, who live in physical comfort and spiritual security, who want to be left alone . . . because we are happy the way we are.

Mad Jesus

One time Jesus got screaming mad. Jesus was causing trouble in the temple, and He was screaming something at the top of His lungs. What would make the God of the universe so incredibly angry? He created and sustains the whole world. What could make Him mad? Jesus went into the temple, and He tore the place up. He was kicking and screaming. Do not think that this was one little psychotic episode in the otherwise perfect life of Jesus. If you remember the account, you will see that He walked in on the first day, looked at everything, observed it, and retired to Bethany. John 5:19 says that Jesus did nothing of His own initiative, but did only what He saw the Father doing. Jesus had perfect permission. He was in perfect agreement with what the Father was feeling and desiring to do when He walked in the next day and started kicking over stalls and whipping the money changers out.

I have heard a lot of people say that Jesus did this because of the cheating that was going on. We do not see Jesus walking up in some fish market and saying, "That scale is unbalanced." This was just not what Jesus was about. He had seen cheating many times during His ministry. No, it was much greater than that, for Israel had many social ills and injustices ... but we do not see Him in any place addressing these, so why here? Jesus Himself tells us in Mark 11:17 as plain as day why He was mad! He yelled at the top of His lungs:

> "My temple is to be a house of prayer for all nations." (Isaiah 56:7)

The problem was not what they were doing, because the buying and selling had to happen for their sacrificial system. This was the system that God Himself had instituted. It was where they were doing it that was really an irritant to God Almighty. They were in the Court of the Gentiles. They had occupied the Court of the Gentiles with their own business.[12] Oh, it was worship business. It was Church business, but this part of the temple had been reserved for the nations to come and worship the one, true God. The place where they could seek Him had been occupied with Jewish worship business. They were "robbing" the world of access to God. There was only one place in the entire world where Gentiles could come

191

and seek God, and the Jews, out of selfishness, had occupied that space with the noises and business of trade.

God told Solomon, after he had built the temple: "I have consecrated this house which you have built to put My name there forever, and My eyes and **My heart** will be there perpetually" (1 Kings 9:3b). Friends, who is the temple today? You and I are. We are the temple of the living God. Even as with the temple of Solomon, God has placed His Name in us. He has adopted us and called us by His Name: *Christ*ian. He also promises His care and concern and watchful blessing upon us, but He did not stop there. He desires the temple of the living God to exemplify His **heart**. He wants to place His heart's passions in us!

As we are the temple of the living God, there is a part of us that is reserved entirely for the Gentiles, those ethne, the nations that have never heard. There is a part that God has set aside that will reveal His heart to the nations. It is time. It is money. It is all those things that you are afraid of giving up. It is part of your life. If we have filled our lives with choir, with church activities, with ministering to our own people, it does not matter how wonderful it is. If we have filled that part in our lives reserved to touch those who have never heard, He wants to come in and kick over some tables.

No Other Plan Under Heaven

God could have written His Gospel on the clouds, but He did not. He chose you and me to be His vessels of communication with the unreached. He could send powerful and immediately obedient angels to proclaim the Good News, but He chose you and me in all our weaknesses, insecurities and foibles, like Moses, to proclaim to the captor and the captives, to sin and hell, slavery and bondage, "Let my people go." S. D. Gordon tells this fictional story, but it illustrates the truth in rare clarity:

> Jesus is walking in heaven one day with Gabriel, talking intently, earnestly. Gabriel is saying, "Master, you died for the whole world down there, did you not?"
>
> "Yes."
>
> "You must have suffered much," with an intent look into the face of Christ with its scars from thorns still visible.
>
> "Yes," again comes the answer quietly, but full of deepest feeling.
>
> "And does the whole world and all her people know about it?"

"Oh, no! Only a few in Palestine know about it so far."

"Well, Master, what's your plan? What have you done about telling the world that you died for, that you *have* died for them? What's your plan?"

"Well," Jesus answer, "I asked Peter, James and John, Andrew, and some more of them down there just to make it the business of their lives to tell others, and the others are to tell others, and the others, and yet others, and still others, until the last man in the farthest circle has heard the good news!"

Gabriel knows people pretty well. He has had more than one contact with the earth. He knows the kind of stuff we are made of. With a sort of hesitating reluctance, as though he could see difficulties in the practical phase of this plan said, "Yes . . . but . . . suppose Peter fails.

Suppose after a while John simply *does not* tell others. Suppose their descendants; their successors away off in the first edge of the twentieth century, get *so busy about things* — some of them proper enough, some maybe not quite so proper — that *they do not* tell others — *what then?*"

And his eyes are big with the intensity of his thought, for he is thinking of — the *suffering*, and he is thinking too of the difference to the man who hasn't been told — "what then?"

Back comes that quiet wondrous voice of Jesus, "Gabriel, *I haven't made any other plans — I'm counting on them.*"[13]

Notes

1. Rev. Dr. James Lee West, Heart of God Ministries, 1998.
2. David Brainerd Woodward, *God, Men and Missions,* (Gospel Light Publications, 1964), pp. 145-146.
3. Hawthorne, Steven, Sermon at Lake View Park Church of the Nazarene, Oklahoma City, OK, Dec. 1993.
4. Frank S. Mead, *Encyclopedia of Religious Quotations,* (London: Peter Davies, Ltd. 1964), p. 112.
5. Bill and Amy Stearns, *Catch the Vision 2000,* (Minneapolis: Bethany House Publishers), 1991.
6. Augustus C. Thompson, *Foreign Missions,* (New York: Charles Scriber's Sons, 1889), p. 66.
7. Ibid., p. 67.
8. Ibid., p. 68.
9. S. D. Gordon, *What It Will Take to Change the World,* (Grand Rapids: Baker Book House, 1979), pp. 82-83.
10. Isobel Kuhn, *Nests Above the Abyss,* (London: China Inland Mission, 1949), p. 209.
11. Gordon, *What It Will Take to Change the World,* p. 82.
12. Ralph Earle, A. Elwood Sanner and Charles L. Childers, *Beacon Bible Commentary Matthew, Mark, Luke* (Kansas City: Beacon Hill Press, 1964), p. 367.
13. S. D. Gordon, *Quiet Talks On Service,* (New York: Fleming H. Revell Company, 1906), pp. 90-92.

appendix:

Storming the Gates

God's heart is being wrung by the despairing cry of some
one of His lost children who might have known His love if
you had been faithful.
A. B. Simpson

Once God's Heart for the nations is understood, we are,
like Paul, constrained by love to communicate His truth.[1]
Meg Crossman

I have been accused of believing that every Christian should be a frontier missionary. Should we all run off and be a Pioneer Missionary? Of course not, however, every Christian is called with the covenant of Abraham. Even today, through us, the God of Abraham desires to less every nation with a restored, reconciled and right relationship with Him. Every Christian is to work toward the fulfillment of the Great Covenant through the Great Commission. We are a people set apart for the service of the King and His purposes on the Earth. He has a unique role for each of us in His Global Rescue operation. Have you discovered your part? Can you say with Paul, "I was not disobedient to the heavenly vision?" (Acts 26:19)

What can you do? If to some degree you now share His heart for the unreached peoples of our world, what should be your response? Though detailed answers are beyond the scope of this book, I do want to share with you some opportunities for you to consider.

Pray: When we look up and see that the harvest is great and the workers are few, Jesus tells us first and foremost to pray!

The harvest truly is great, but the laborers are few; therefore
pray to the Lord of the harvest to send out laborers into His
harvest (Luke 10:2).

The sheer size of the task remaining in missions should drive us to our knees begging the Lord of the Harvest to awaken and send forth a mighty army of harvesters into His field, that none would perish, but all would be brought into His storehouse! Ross Paterson writes, "The logical extension of embracing God's heart for another people or nation is that we should pray for them."[3]

Some helps to your prayer life: Get the Frontlines magazine from Heart of God Ministries (www.HeartofGod.com) or other frontier missions magazines. These include many news items and stories that will help you know how to pray for missionaries and the unreached peoples.

Go: Be careful when you pray! If you are following along in your Bible (Lk. 10:2-3), after Jesus tells them to pray, He sends them out! If you have felt His call on your life and know that you are to go where the name of Christ has never been proclaimed, then obey today! Tell your pastor/discipler of your desire, and they will assist to confirm this call of God on your life.

Practically, begin now to acquire the skills necessary to be a good missionary. Cultivate your passion for souls through eager evangelism and discipleship. If you have not led small groups, begin now. Ask your pastor to disciple you in these basic skills.

Along with the callings, you need the giftings and anointing to match, so begin now to ardently seek the fullness of His Spirit. Jesus told His disciples to go into all the earth after they were filled with the power of His Spirit! Don't leave home without it!

When you are ready, talk to us at Heart of God Ministries or another frontier mission agency for an application.

Whether you are young or old, He is not mistaken in calling you. If you have skills in the business world or are a teacher, perhaps He will call you to be a "tent-maker" as Paul was, supporting his ministry through work. Many countries that are closed to traditional church planters are wide open to people who have skills. I know that right now teachers are in high demand in China.

Before you go, get training! There are several ways to get it. We at HGM have Beautiful Feet Boot Camp, a five-month intensive, training institute available for those who are about to go to the unreached. Too many run off to the field without proper preparation and return prematurely in emotional, physical and spiritual shambles. BFBC is an essential step in fulfilling God's plan through you. (See Appendix II Beautiful Feet Boot Camp.)

Send: This is not nearly as much fun as going. It can also be infinitely harder, but if you know He is calling you to stay, then He will give you the grace to send. Sending is as crucial as going. Romans 10 tells us that the unreached are that way for lack of a preacher/ missionary. There are no missionaries because there are no senders. The plan of God on planet earth is that some stay back and prayerfully and financially support those who go to the front. These rare and sacrificial people resist the pressure of culture, friends and family and live a simple life . . . that the unreached, those who are in prisons of death, may have life and life abundant!

I know of many missionaries who are gifted, called, and even have completed training at Beautiful Feet Boot Camp but cannot go, because they are lacking those who would send them. Our participation by sending missionaries to the front of this spiritual conflict is necessary for our own blessing. If we don't obey this element of His call, not only will the unreached suffer, but also we will miss out.

> If you send them forward on their journey in a manner
> worthy of God, you will do well, because they went forth
> for His name's sake, taking nothing from the Gentiles
> [ethne]. (3 John 6,7)

Esther was chosen as Queen, and in her position of influence and relative affluence, she was the appointed savior of her people. The Jews were condemned to death, and she was the only voice that could stop Haman's plans of genocide. Mordecai came to Esther and asked her to risk her life and approach the king on behalf of her people.

> "Who knows if you have attained royalty for such a time
> as this?" (Esther 4:14)

Dear reader, who knows if you have attained riches and wealth for such a time as this? Who knows if you have attained status, position, and education for such a time as this? The peoples of the world are condemned to sure death, unless we, like Esther, risk our comforts and well being on their behalf.

Some Ideas:
- Find out the average income of a missionary. If it is lower than your salary, adjust to it over a period of months. Perhaps cut $100 out of your budget each month or every

two months until your level of living matches. Give what you save to a frontier missionary or frontier mission agency. Another variation on this "downwardly mobile" idea is to consult a financial planner and get help setting a specific plan to decrease debt and increase your giving to frontier missions.

• Shop carefully for every item. Find out the lowest price and give away what was saved!

• Collect your loose change daily, count it out monthly and deposit it. Then send a check for that amount to a frontier mission agency focused on finishing the task among the unreached.

• Use your vacation time to visit the missionaries (delivering gifts, giving breaks from the kids, etc.) and go on crucial prayer walks assisting the missionaries in this holy struggle against the kingdoms of darkness.

• Get the book *Serving As Senders* by Neil Pirolo, a great guide to being the best sender you can be, both personally and as a church.

Mobilize: The unreached need advocates who will plead their case in churches and meetings today. Most commonly, this is an informal activity, as you influence your friends and family, hand off articles of interest and remind people to pray.

Part-time and full-time mobilizers are needed in many agencies. We, at HGM, need people to sponsor Concerts of Prayer, Heart of God Seminars (This book was based on this seminar. It is an excellent way in a few short hours to bring your congregation, small group, missions council, district, or home fellowship up to speed with God's amazing plan for the world.), small group studies of books like this one that focus on God's passion for the nations. WWII was won in large measure because of the outstanding job mobilizers did in calling the country to war. If we are to finish this job in our generation, it will require a corps of mobilizers who make a clear call.

The Gates are Coming!
If ever there was a season for heroism, it is in our generation. In a world where there still exist peoples locked away in dungeons of darkness, we have the Gospel of power to free them from bondage. It is time for us to

storm the gates of hell. Jesus told Peter that the Gates of Hell could not resist the Bride of Christ. Some may think that we are guaranteed security from the strength of hell by this statement, but Jesus is promising His power to overcome hell's grasp on the peoples of the world.

How many of us have been attacked by a gate? Gates just stand there as an obstacle and a barricade to overcome. I have never heard of gates charging the enemy. We are the ones that are to charge gates. We have divine power and promise to charge them and overcome their resistance. Whatever the form resistance has taken, governmental restrictions or the stronghold of culture and religion, we will prevail! In order to achieve victory, we must attack! Through Abraham and his spiritual descendants, God promised to bless all the peoples of the world. But the first step was a proactive responsibility to take this blessing to them. First, we go to the stronghold of resistance, the gate of our enemy, and charge, in order to free those captive behind it. Still Islam, Hinduism, Buddhism and Idolatry enslave two billion people. We must take the fight to them! Only then will peoples be blessed with the blessing of Abraham.

> Your seed shall possess the gates of their enemies. And in
> your seed all the nations of the earth shall be blessed,
> because you have obeyed my voice (Genesis 22:17b-18).

The exciting reality of this cosmic conflict for the tongues, tribes and nations of our world will not be won without our active participation. He wants to be victorious through us, His Bride. That final victory over His enemies, bringing salvation to those sitting in darkness, happens through His Church. The God of peace will soon crush Satan under your feet (Rom. 16:20). We are His Body on earth; we are His hands and feet! The ultimate blow against Satan and his grip over the remaining unreached is through you and me. Jesus has all power in heaven and on earth; He has the victory over death and the grave; He promises to be with us to the very end; now it is our part to GO! What a great time to be alive! If we are faithful with the resources in personnel, time, energy and finances, we will see a righteous harvest of worshipers from every nation. You have been chosen by your Creator to live during this important time. You have been given a position of wealth and honor and insight (compared to the rest of the world's people). Now what is the responsibility attached? To whom much has been given, much will be required.

Notes:
1. Meg Crossman, *Worldwide Perspectives*, (Pasadena: William Carey Library, 1995) p. 15-1.

appendix two:

Beautiful Feet Boot Camp
Missionary Training Institute of Heart of God Ministries

Heart of God Ministries has been called by God to stand in the gap between those who desperately need to hear about Jesus and those who are being called to go. HGM's ambition is to take the Good News to places it has never been. This is the same desire that the Apostle Paul expressed when he said, "My ambition is to go still further where Christ has not yet been named." (Romans 15:20) There are still approximately 6,000 groups of people that have no Church. These unreached people groups are the final frontiers to which Heart of God Ministries is called.

HGM's team sending policy is great news for all who have felt called into missions, yet don't fit the classical stereotype of "preaching prophet." Recognizing the excellence of transplanting the body of Christ, HGM will commission several missionaries together. This allows members of all ages and backgrounds to pool their talents and spiritual gifts and overcome individual weaknesses. Through these shared strengths, HGM believes each team will have the combination of gifts needed to effectively reach their target people — even if the individuals do not. Also, this becomes a model for the indigenous Church of how to love and care for its members. When one member falls down or is wounded, in love and support, the members of the team can care for him/her.

The Boot Camp
Any one who has been to the mission field understands the difficulties in adjustment, culture shock, language learning and spiritual warfare. The missionaries must be prepared before they leave. So God has called HGM to sponsor a five month training institute for this purpose. All the training at the institute (BFBC) is geared toward making the student a pioneer missionary able to penetrate unreached peoples and plant the Church of Jesus Christ. Some missionaries currently on the field bemoan the fact that they did not go through this vital preparation.

Yeah, but Five Months?
With the pressing needs of our world and thousands slipping into eternity every day, we are anxious not to keep missionaries in the "just training" process longer than necessary. However, we understand that this five months is the bare necessity

and not really enough.Therefore, while on the field, those missionaries serving with HGM will continue to receive education via course offerings and itinerant "coaches" visiting as a resource and support.

The time one takes to train is sacrifice. It is no surprise for a brain surgeon to expect years of training, yet the task of taking Jesus to the unreached is infinitely more important with eternal consequences. (The brain surgeon rarely has an enemy in the operating room like we do who desires to cause him to make a mistake and kill the patient. We do.)

Boot Camp
This intense training is undertaken immediately prior to departure for the "front" and is therefore geared to be extremely relevant to the missionaries. "Boot Camp" is a most appropriate title for this institute.

It is imperative that our missionaries be sent with adequate crosscultural preparation but most importantly having true intimacy with Christ. Theological education, though helpful, is not an instant qualifier for the mission field, nor does it guarantee that Christ is reflected in the person's life. Therefore, two arenas: spiritual formation and cross-cultural ministry, are central to Beautiful Feet Boot Camp.

Perfect Missionaries
Though the training cannot guarantee the "production" of perfect cross-cultural missionaries, students will be exposed to the best information available in cultural anthropology, contextualization (presenting the Gospel in culturally relevant and sensitive ways), linguistics, etc. in order to sensitize them to the dynamics of presenting the Gospel cross-culturally. Our desire is to equip the missionaries with some coping skills that will lay a crucial framework for life-long, on-the-job learning and application. Five weeks of training will be spent in an intensive cultural immersion, living and studying in another culture.Students will be getting the best practical hands on training available.

The Good Seed
Students can learn very effectively how to communicate and live cross culturally, but if they do not have the content of the communication, the effort will be in vain. It is very important that missionaries be taking the true "Good Seed." They need to know what to contextualize as well as how. Missiology without an emphasis on the primary issue of being connected with Jesus will result in empty pragmatism and activity.

Therefore, Beautiful Feet Boot Camp will put a strong emphasis on the personal relationship with Jesus and learning to hear His voice. We have the goal of doing and saying only that which is Spirit led — thus embodying "holiness, without which no one will see the Lord."

The training is realistic preparation for the problems that will be faced on the field in another culture. In teams, students discover hearing the Lord, learning together, helping one another, being the body of Christ, being creative together, etc. Teachers at the institute are always available, facilitating discipleship, and helping in the "healing" of those in need.

Contact Us

Expenses are kept as low as possible and include room, board, cultural immersion, and tuition. The course of study is a full five months. Though there is a cost in being obedient to His calling, it is nothing compared to the joy which is yours in Christ Jesus as you take His love and freedom to those who still sit in the lands of darkness. If you have heard your Master in what you have read, contact us today for more information:

Heart of God Ministries
3720 S. Hiwassee Rd.
Choctaw, OK 73020
(405) 737-9446
www.heartofgod.com
hgm@heartofgod.com

Encourage Others
Through This Book

Copies of *Passion for the Heart of God* are sold
for whatever you can afford.

Call today to order your copies at:
(405) 737-9446

Or complete the following form and mail it with payment to:
Heart of God Ministries
ATTN: HGM Publishing
3720 S. Hiwassee Rd.
Choctaw, OK 73020

☐ Yes! Please send me _____ copies of
Passion for the Heart of God
at US $ _____ each.

☐ Yes, God is calling me to go!
Please send me more information about
Beautiful Feet Boot Camp.

☐ Please send me the magazine, Frontlines.

PLEASE PRINT

Name_____

Address_____

City_____State_____ Zip/Postal Code_____

Country_____ Telephone (____)_____

Email_____

Total payment enclosed: US $_____

Make checks payable to Heart of God Ministries.

Passion for the Heart of God
is also available as a four-hour, live seminar.

Contact HGM for information at:
Heart of God Ministries
3720 S. Hiwassee Rd. Choctaw, OK 73020
(405) 737-9446
www.heartofgod.com
hgm@heartofgod.com

"It was one of the most moving/challenging presentations our people have experienced. I expect lifetime changes of perspective to result. Several have shared how they have been greatly impacted by God's love for His Son, His Son's Bride and the lost. God's concern for the whole world was powerfully noted by many."

Rev. Bob Luhn, Pastor, Othello, WA

"Excellent presentation. Eye, mind and heart opening to the heart of God for the lost peoples of the earth."

Rev. Merrill Williams, Pastor, Manhattan, KS

"All missionary presidents and councils should take this seminar. I can think of no better method to capture the zeal and the passion necessary to effectively mobilize our churches into mission. This should be a priority activity of all missionary societies."

Dr. Howard Culbertson, Missionary, Professor and Author

"The Heart of God Seminar is a must event. To finally have an opportunity to zoom through the Bible seeing how our God is a missionary God is truly eye-opening. The Bible from cover to cover shows that God's concern is to win all peoples to Jesus. Nothing like the Heart of God Seminar illustrates this as clearly and succinctly in an exciting and fun way."

Dr. James L. West, Executive Director, Heart of God Ministries and Author

"The Heart of God Seminar was presented to our church board and their spouses. I was blown away with the concept of looking at the Bible as one book that tells about God's heart for the peoples who have never heard of Jesus. This seminar has made a significant difference in how I look at the Bible, missions, and my response to the "original" Great Commission."

Mrs. Annette Ferrell, Church Office Administrator

"I heartily recommend the Heart of God Seminar to any pastor and congregation that desires to find God's ultimate priority for his church."

Rev. Dennis King, Pastor, Potsdam, NY